D1306885

THINKING
THROUGH OUR
FAITH

*Theology for
Twenty-first-Century
Christians*

C. DAVID GRANT

ABINGDON PRESS
NASHVILLE

THINKING THROUGH OUR FAITH:
THEOLOGY FOR TWENTY-FIRST-CENTURY CHRISTIANS

This book is printed on recycled, acid-free, elemental-chlorine-free paper.

Library of Congress Cataloging-in-Publication Data

Grant, C. David, 1949–
    Thinking through our faith : theology for twenty-first-century Christians / C. David
Grant.
        p.   cm.
    Includes bibliographical references and index.
    ISBN 0-687-01727-0 (alk. paper)
    1. Theology, Doctrinal.   I. Title.
BT78.G66   1998
230'.76—dc21   97-35076
                                                                                    CIP

98 99 00 01 02 03 04 05 06 07 — 10 9 8 7 6 5 4 3 2 1

MANUFACTURED IN THE UNITED STATES OF AMERICA

For my parents,
Charles and Adeline Grant

The more concrete objects of most men's religion, the deities whom they worship, are known to them only in idea.

—William James

CONTENTS

*E*ach of us is shaped by our historical situation. We are who we are largely because of the context in which we live. And we can only understand people in the past if we come to grips with the ways they thought and the ideas and images available to them in their historical situation.

This is no less true of the author of this work. This book is the result of my own life's context. How I think, how I experience life, how I learn, how I live—all these are shaped by my past and present contexts.

I cut my theological teeth as a teenager in the Methodist Youth Fellowship of University Park United Methodist Church in Dallas, Texas. Several faculty members of Perkins School of Theology were members of that church, and our youth ministers during the 1960s were drawn from the students at Perkins. There I first learned that hard thinking about Christian faith was a central and exciting dimension of one's spiritual life. I would not be doing what I'm doing today were it not for that congregation's witness to the viability and value of an intellectual approach to faith.

Four teachers have especially shaped my theology. I sat in the classrooms of James H. Ware at Austin College, Schubert M. Ogden at SMU's Perkins School of Theology, and Gordon D. Kaufman at Harvard University. Though none, I suspect, will agree with everything I say, their influences lurk behind each and every sentence; so does the theological vision of H. Richard Niebuhr. I never sat in his classroom, nor did I ever meet him.

9

But his writings have taught me much about a way of seeing Christian faith; those who are familiar with his work will see his influence, too, in the following pages.

I am privileged to be associated with a congregation of Christians that believes in serious thinking about faith. Many of the ideas in this book were originally presented in adult church school classes and special lecture series at First United Methodist Church of Fort Worth, Texas, and I am indebted to the many folks there who over the years asked questions of and made comments on my ideas. I also want to thank Dr. Justin Tull, and the congregation of Oak Lawn United Methodist Church of Dallas, Texas, whose kind invitation to deliver the 1996 Albert C. Outler Lectures gave me the opportunity to present the material that now, in modified form, constitutes chapters 4, 5, and 6 of this book.

Several colleagues have read portions of the manuscript and offered very helpful suggestions. I thank Professors Rudolf Brun, Nadia Lahutsky, and Daryl Schmidt for their comments as well as for many hours of conversations over the issues about which this book is concerned.

My wife, Deborah, and my three daughters, Carolyn, Amanda, and Allison, have had to put up with an absentee husband and father for far too many weekends while this book has taken shape. But their patient kindness and love have made the task much less onerous than it otherwise might have been.

I learned little theology from my parents. But what I did learn has shaped my thinking about God as profoundly as all the volumes of theology I've read. For in our home, I experienced and learned the meaning of unconditional love. For that lesson, I am forever grateful, and I dedicate this book to them.

*A*s an avid participant in my Methodist church's youth group, I enjoyed singing the gospel song "Give Me That Old-Time Religion." Although my church had what for Methodists was a high liturgy and a taste for hymns more in line with Isaac Watts and Charles Wesley than Fannie J. Crosby, we would on occasion sing the "other" hymns and songs at retreats and church camps. It was at such an event that I learned this gospel classic.

I still enjoy singing a close harmony rendition of this song, but I do so with more theologically attuned ears. The song's message implies that old-time religion is better than new-time religion; that what was good for our parents and grandparents ought to be good enough for us. Its lyrics surely raise in us a nostalgia for a simpler faith held in simpler times. But why do we want old-time religion? Would we nostalgically join in singing "Give me that old-time transportation," or "Give me that old-time medicine," or "Give me those old-time communications"? Why are we willing to settle for a faith that is less than contemporary, that ignores recent advances in thinking, when we aren't willing to settle for anything less than the most current thinking in so many other areas of our life?

I shall argue in the following pages that we must be Christians in *our* day and in *our* time. To be faithful to God requires that we live out that faith in *our* contemporary world, not the world of our parents, or grandparents, or even of Jesus' first disciples. Not only is old-time religion simply hollow for many of us today, it denies God's creative goodness by suggesting that we should strive to be people of an earlier time and place, even though God created us to be persons in this time and place. To be responsible Christians we must take our contemporary world seriously, knowing as much as we can about the best thinking being done in all realms of thought. To do otherwise is to slight not only ourselves but God's creative goodness.

Three aspects of current thinking seem especially relevant for rethinking the nature of our faith, and these will be the focus of part 1. First, the rise of historical thinking over the past two centuries has profoundly affected all of Western thought, from science to literature. The story of Christian theology in this century is largely the story of the sea change of thinking that inevitably accompanied the recognition that human life is inextricably embedded in history. Thinking Christians must face the issues raised by the rise of historical thought. These will be addressed in chapter 1.

Second, Christians cannot avoid taking modern science seriously, since it, more than any other factor, shapes today's cultural worldview. Science and its child we call technology are most responsible for the physical changes in our lives that form the environment in which we live and think. But the advances of science have also profoundly affected the images that we have of ourselves and the cosmos of which we are but an infinitesimal part. New theories of the origin of the universe, as well as new theories concerning the operations of the smallest cells within our brains, must be explored by Christians thinking through what it means to be created by God in God's image. The role of science in shaping modern worldviews will be the topic of chapter 2.

Third, we Christians must take seriously the contemporary discussion of pluralism, for the recognition of multiplicity and diversity in our cultures, lives, and thought is a central characteristic of our age. How do we take pluralism seriously in our religious practice and theological thought? The recognition and appreciation by Christians of the other great world religious traditions have significantly changed the ways we think about

God's revelations to humankind and forced many of us to rethink our inherited notions of missions in the non-Western world. In a world that is increasingly smaller as a result of communication technology and rapid transportation, we today must confront the issue of other religions in ways that our forebears never even imagined.

And yet the question of pluralism is not limited only to the plurality of religions in the world. It also arises as we look to the diversity within Christianity itself. In former times, denominations often held that their way of being Christian was the only right way. Then in the middle of this century the church union movement suggested that the only right thing for the divided churches to do was to reunite as one body of Christ. Today, however, we recognize the intractable character of diversity and how multiculturalism can contribute to a more profound understanding of human life. So too we must ask how within the fold of Christianity we can accept the diversity that makes up the body of Christ. These issues will be addressed in chapter 3.

In part 2, I will explore important aspects of our faith that must be rethought in light of the changed context outlined in part 1. So chapter 4 tackles the question of the Bible, and the impact of history, science, and pluralism on the ways we can today appropriate and use this foundational document while yet recognizing its human and historical character. In chapter 5 I turn to the question of Jesus Christ and how we might think about him today, given the new view of the Bible that I think is required. When we think of Jesus Christ, it is the biblical images of Jesus of which we think. Our faith, just as the faith of those Christians before us, is based on trust in those biblical images and what they reveal to us of God, not of the irretrievable historical Jesus. New literary approaches to the Bible enable us to get out of the box that mere historical criticism put us in and, I think, help us recover a sense of relating to those pictures in authentic and intelligible ways.

In chapter 6 I address the question that has driven this whole study: How are we to think about God today? I shall argue that our thought about God is fundamental to the whole way we see ourselves as Christians and the world in which we dwell as God's creation. Indeed, it is precisely through our thinking that we relate to God; even our experience of God is based on our thought of God. A way for us to relate *with* God today is to think *through* to God.

In what follows I shall be developing and arguing for a particular option for thinking about Christians' faith; but I recognize that it will not have universal appeal. I want to develop a way of thinking about God that will appeal to those who want to take seriously the contemporary intellectual and social world and who believe that God is worthy of continual rethinking in light of new developments and new knowledge. But I am far from claiming that only those who think about Christianity in these terms are the true believers and all others wrong. I propose to lay out a way for Christian faith today, a way that takes seriously the role of thinking. I acknowledge that it is not the only available way of faith and that many conservative Christians will find it inadequate and unorthodox. But I hope to make the case that it is a feasible option for Christians' theology today, for God's all-encompassing reality is larger than any of our particular attempts to understand and live within it.

PART ONE

COMPONENTS OF
CONTEMPORARY
THOUGHT

CHAPTER ONE

THE IMPACT OF HISTORICAL THINKING

Science's impact on our world today is obvious. Even the most conservative Christians recognize that technology has changed, if not the message, at least the media for proclaiming the gospel. During this century, the appearance of first, radios, next, televisions, and then computers in our homes demonstrates how much we've benefited from the fruits of science. As a result, we live very different lives from those of our forebears. And as we'll see in the next chapter, we cannot view the world apart from those fruits. Christians who take seriously the intellectual developments of the past three centuries have to confront the disciplines of natural science and what we have learned of our world through them.

But another intellectual revolution of modern times is just as foundational for contemporary thinking and that is the revolution in historical consciousness. This revolution, though born of the same spirit as the scientific revolution, has come to stand in awkward tension with it. As science has succeeded in developing an almost universal method for discovering the empirical world we live in, the revolution in historical consciousness has shown us that the social and intellectual worlds we inhabit are incorrigibly culturally and historically specific. This discovery has had even greater impact than science on Christians and their faith. Indeed it has shaped the very foundations of contemporary belief. Most of the disputes and controversies among Christians, from dogmas about Christ to policies regarding homosexuals, are rooted in this revolution in historical consciousness that began in the Enlightenment and culminated in the nineteenth century. Christians who seek a faith continuous with contemporary intellectual thought must come to grips with historical consciousness. What is historical consciousness and how did it come about?

THE RISE OF CRITICAL HISTORY

Historical consciousness has two components, the rise of critical history and the awareness of historicism. Both of these components came to full fruition in the late–nineteenth century, although the groundwork for them was laid as far back as the Renaissance and Reformation.

On the face of it, the claim that the discipline of history only matured in the last century is hard to believe. After all, human interest in the past is found even in the most ancient civilizations. Narratives about the past form the earliest of our literature in the West. The Greek epic poems of Homer, the *Iliad* and the *Odyssey*, written in the eighth century B.C.E. concerning earlier events in the twelfth century B.C.E.; the *Torah* of ancient Israel, written beginning in the tenth century B.C.E. about events at least as early as the fifteenth century B.C.E.; the many hieroglyphs of ancient Egypt preserving the deeds and accomplishments of ancient pharaohs; and cuneiform tablets from ancient Mesopotamia recounting the stories of the very beginning of human being and the struggles among the gods that brought about the world—all these ancient writings show a profound interest in the past.

But of course we do not consider them to be histories in the modern sense of the word. We recognize them to contain much legend and mythology. But the very fact that we are able to recognize these other components in such ancient works is itself the result of using modern historical-critical judgment.

Most historical narratives in the ancient and medieval world depended on the uncritical use of narrative reports from others for information that the author could not furnish from his or her own firsthand experience. Although impressive and important historical works resulted from this method—one need only think of the works of persons such as Herodotus (fifth-century B.C.E. Greece), Tacitus (first- and second-century C.E. Rome), or the important early Christian historian Eusebius of Caesarea (third- and fourth-century C.E. Palestine)—we recognize today that a simple reporting of what someone tells us does not make for adequate historical work. The testimony of those whose reports we recount must be critically evaluated, must be judged as to whether we think them credible. A critical historian goes behind the accounts of eyewitnesses to make a judgment as to whether the account is reliable or not. It is this taking responsibility for judging the testimony that most differentiates critical history from the practices of its predecessors.[1]

Ernst Troeltsch, a late-nineteenth- and early-twentieth-century German theologian, captures this modern spirit of critical history in three principles he lays out in a very important 1898 essay, "Historical and Dogmatic Method in Theology" (1991). His first principle, the principle of criticism, recognizes that all judgments about events in the past are judgments of probability, and all judgments of probability are open to reassessment and correction. This principle, which likewise operates in the natural and social sciences, is a fundamental part of our thinking today. No judgment about past actions is absolutely certain, and no proposition about the past is to be accepted simply on the basis of authority. We may reach a very high degree of probability in our statements about the past; nonetheless, there is always room for such statements to be reassessed in light of new evidence.

Take for example the statement, "Lee Harvey Oswald assassinated President Kennedy in 1963." This judgment has a high

---

1. See Collingwood 1993 for an excellent account of the rise of critical history.

degree of probability, so much so that most historians, and indeed most of the general population, accept this statement as true. But it is not absolutely certain. Some people argue that someone else fired the shot that killed Kennedy, perhaps someone working with Oswald on the grassy knoll in Dealey Plaza. Because of this principle of criticism, it is important that new theories, with their evidence and arguments, be brought forth and examined, for there is always a possibility that our generally accepted historical judgments are wrong and must be corrected.

Let's take an example from biblical studies. Generations upon generations of Christians accepted that Paul wrote all the letters in the New Testament that identify him as their author. Take the Pastoral Letters—1 and 2 Timothy and Titus. We have fragmentary evidence that at least some early Christians outside the mainstream did not include one or more of these letters among their collections of Paul's letters. But by the end of the second century, mainstream Christianity accepted these three letters as genuinely Pauline (Collins 1988, 89). It was only in the nineteenth century that scholars compiled evidence that these were not from the hand of Paul. Similarly, assumptions about the Pauline authorship of Ephesians, Colossians, and 2 Thessalonians came into question at about the same time. New Testament scholars today largely agree that these particular letters were not written by Paul. But any new evidence to the contrary would be seriously examined. This is the way the principle of criticism works.

Prior to the rise of critical history, *authority* played a large role in historical judgments. These books carry introductory salutations that state they are from Paul. On the basis of the simple acceptance of authority, Christians for centuries never questioned these claims. Indeed, it would not have entered the minds of Christians to think otherwise. With the rise of critical history, however, scholars began to question the Pauline authorship on the grounds of inconsistencies in style and content with other genuinely Pauline letters. In the short period between 1792 and 1824, New Testament scholars raised questions about the

Pauline authorship of every letter generally accepted today to be pseudo-Pauline, that is, written by one of Paul's followers but in the name of Paul (Collins 1988). It was precisely the principle of criticism that made it possible for nineteenth-century biblical scholars to ask the question that early Christians had not been able to ask.

Troeltsch's second principle of historical method is the principle of *analogy*. The historian begins with the assumption that the past is analogous to the present, or more precisely, the historian is to understand the past by analogy with his or her experience in the present.

This principle works in conjunction with the principle of criticism: claims that are consistent with our own experience tend to be accepted initially with a higher probability than those that are not consistent with our own experience.

If, for instance, a student reported to me that he had been involved in a traffic accident just off campus last night, my initial reaction would be to accept that testimony at face value. I have seen traffic accidents and even have been involved in traffic accidents. Should the student claim this accident as the reason he missed an examination, I could easily check his testimony by corroborating his story with police reports, other witnesses' accounts, and the like. I might even be initially suspicious of his report, because students have lied to me in the past about their reasons for missing an examination. My previous experiences become the analogy on which to base judgments about new claims. All this is part and parcel of the way most of us think in our daily lives.

But what if, instead, the student came and reported that he had been abducted by aliens from Mars for an overnight tour of the solar system, and this happened while he was driving alone in the country so that there were no witnesses to corroborate his story? Most of us would agree that such a story would be highly improbable because alien abductions are events most people don't experience. Indeed, the stories of those who claim to have had such experiences usually don't stand up to investigative scrutiny. So we quite legitimately require a great deal more corroborating evidence for judging such claims that fall outside areas of analogous experience than for those that do not.

Our modern historical consciousness here converges with modern science, for the latter unquestionably shapes the way that we understand our experiences today. For example, our understanding of disease processes has undergone great transformation in our century. Illnesses have physical causes and we have isolated many of these causes in parasitic, bacterial, and viral infections. Recently, we've identified other diseases as having genetic origins, and yet others as arising from diet and lifestyle. Much yet remains to be learned about these processes, but what we have already discovered is one of the impressive achievements of modern medicine.

When we make historical judgments on past claims of healings, we must do so from our own knowledge of medicine. When we assess an ancient or medieval account of a healing, we must interpret it in conscious analogy to our modern knowledge of medicine, not on the basis of the author's interpretation that the disease resulted from spirit-possession or imbalanced body humors. Past accounts of healings *are* to be taken seriously by the historian, but such reports cannot be accepted *uncritically*. Just as most of us today would find it almost beyond belief if someone were to report that an amputated leg had miraculously grown back overnight after taking a pill, so we are also skeptical when reports of regrown limbs come from the ancient world. Just as we might seek an explanation, not of the reported phenomenon but of why a person would report such a thing, so also must the critical historians find explanations of the past that mesh with their contemporary knowledge. Let's take another example. Shooting stars, we now know, are very different objects from fixed stars. They are meteorites, pieces of cosmic rock that glow brightly due to the friction caused by their entry into our atmosphere, whereas stars are trillions of miles away and glow from the burning of hydrogen and helium in great fusion reactions. A historian who reads an ancient account describing a star falling from heaven understands that what the witness describes is not really a star falling from heaven but a meteorite. She can appreciate why the ancient person thought it to be a star falling from heaven, but she cannot accept the ancient description uncritically. And since natural science plays such an important role in our modern understanding of the world and the natural events that affect us, so it must play a crucial role in the historian's attempt to understand the past. It is the analogies to our present experience and present understanding of the world that give historians a basis for making critical judgments.

The third principle Troeltsch uses to describe critical history is the principle of *mutual interrelation* or *correlation*. All events form a web in which each event has a context in which it occurs, and each event thereafter becomes part of the context for events that follow. To understand an event historically is to understand it by looking at the context in which it appears and the effects it has on events after it. No event stands isolated from other events. All history is an interconnected web of relationships such that our understanding of any event within it is increased in light of what we understand of the whole context in which it occurs.

A good example of this principle in action is the attention historians are now giving to the social context in which Jesus lived and in which early Christianity arose. Historians have come to understand how important the social context of first-century Palestinian Judaism is to any understanding of the rise of Christianity. Jesus lived and taught in a specific context; to understand what he taught and who he was, we must understand the web of interconnections in which he lived. Likewise, to understand the spread of Christianity in the Roman world requires that we study the social context of that Roman world, what Roman subjects did, what they believed, how they lived, and what they owned. Paul's mission to the Gentiles occurred in the Hellenistic context of the Roman world.

The principles of critical history significantly shape our modern consciousness of the past. Critical history is so universally practiced in the academy that we often fail to recognize how differently our forebears approached the past. But there is another dimension to the study of history that also influences how we think today. We've come to recognize how humans are significantly shaped by the particular cultures of which they are a part. As historians critically study the past they also discover how greatly the past shapes present beliefs and values: *to be human is to have a history and a culture.* This discovery of the sociohistorical character of being human is the discovery of our human *historicity.*[2]

Unlike other animals, for whom instinct plays the most central role in their specific behaviors, humans are shaped largely by cultures that are passed down through learned languages and other symbol systems. Human knowledge is cumulative. The intellectual, moral, and spiritual wisdom gained by our forebears is preserved in our cultures. Since the advent of written language, humans have evolved a means of very specifically recording the cumulative wisdom of their pasts, and a visit to any large library leaves one awestruck at the immense amount of knowledge that has been discovered, created, and preserved. The whole of our educational process, from the basic acquisition of language in toddlers to doctoral research at universities, arises out of our human need to preserve, pass on, and create our cultures.

But here is where our cumulative knowledge has led us to recognize the particularity of our cultures. As long as cultures were distinct and isolated, one culture's view of its world was assumed to be *the* world. (I use *world* here in the sense of the Greek word *cosmos*, to designate the whole of one's experienced and conceived reality.) Over the past two centuries, however, improved

---

2. H. Richard Niebuhr (1941) and Gordon Kaufman (1993) develop the idea of human historicity in their work.

means of travel and improved communications have made us aware of the diverse cultures that inhabit our planet; cultures based on different languages, different moral systems, different intellectual standards, and different religious traditions. We can no longer assume that our understanding of our world is *the* world. We must recognize that our understanding is *our* understanding and that there are cultures today that see and experience the world differently from how we do.

To be human is to live, think, and act in a particular culture. Indeed, we may say that to be human is to have a culture. But there is not a single common human culture. Analogously, we can say that to be human is to speak a language. But this does not entail that there is a common human language. Languages are diverse. Many are closely related due to their historical derivations. But a language is not a neutral set of symbols that describes a fully completed world that is objectively independent of the users of language. If it were, translation from one language to another would be a relatively simple procedure of mapping one set of words onto another by comparing the common objective referents of the words. Translation is never that simple because languages are *constitutive* as well as *descriptive*; that is, languages *shape* as well as simply *describe* our experiences. Languages contain culture: as long as there are different cultures there will be different languages and vice versa.

This close relationship between language and culture is well illustrated in history. For Christians, the very fact that the New Testament is written in koine Greek, the common language of trade and commerce of the eastern Mediterranean world of the Roman Empire, itself indicates how deeply Hellenistic culture is imbedded in the earliest Christian documents. Jesus and the earliest Christians were natives of Galilee, a Jewish enclave in northern Palestine whose inhabitants spoke Aramaic, a Semitic language learned by the Jews during the exile to Babylon that came to replace Hebrew as the everyday language. Yet the documents contained in the New Testament were all written in Greek. Why the shift? Was this simply an accident of convenience? Not at all. It represents the fact that Christianity as we know it quickly moved out of its Palestinian setting and spread into the Mediterranean world, a world for which the lingua franca, the language used to communicate among different peoples, was Greek. As Christianity spread into the geographical world of the Roman Empire and into the thought world of Hellenism, it took on characteristics of that cultural world. And the conversion of the Roman emperor Constantine to Christianity in the first quarter of the fourth century, followed by the establishment of Christianity as the official religion of the Roman Empire under Theodosius I in the last quarter of the fourth century, sealed the cultural directions that this new religion would take in its further developments.

Take, for example, the categories from Greek philosophical thought that came to define the orthodox Christian doctrine of the relation between Jesus and God. By the time of Paul's letters, and certainly by the time of the gospels' composition, Christians had already begun to proclaim that Jesus was the Son of God. The great commission at the end of Matthew's Gospel commands the disciples to "go therefore and make disciples of all nations, baptizing them in the name of the Father and of the Son and of the Holy Spirit" (28:19). This threefold distinction later evolved into orthodox trinitarian dogma. A crucial step in the development occurred in 325 C.E. at the Council of Nicea when Greek philosophical categories were invoked to explain the relation between the Son and the Father.

The question of the exact relation between the Father and the Son was in debate for decades prior to the Council of Nicea. But the issues came to a head in the debates between Arius and Athanasius in the years just prior to the Council. Arius, a pastor in Alexandria, Egypt, argued that the Son or Logos was among the first of God's creatures. Appealing to the passages in Proverbs in which Wisdom is described as being created at the beginning of the Lord's work (8:22), Arius and his followers came to understand that Jesus was the incarnation of a divine being derived from God but distinct from God. The defender of what came to be the orthodox position, Athanasius, also of Alexandria, argued vehemently against the subordination of the Logos or Son to the Father. For Athanasius, the Son was begotten of the Father but not made by the Father. The Son was not a creature but was eternally with the Father.

This controversy troubled the newly converted Constantine; as a result he called a council of bishops from his empire to settle the issue. They met in the year 325 C.E. in Nicea in Asia Minor. The council decided in favor of Athanasius's view and condemned Arius's. What's important about the decision in light of our discussion is not the decision but the *language* used to decide the issue. The council decided that the Son was to be understood as *homoousios* with the Father or, as we translate this Greek phrase, the Son is "of the same substance" with the Father. Nowhere in scripture is the relation between God and Jesus described in these terms of substance. Indeed, the category of substance derives from Greek philosophical thought and its concern with Being and the attributes of Being. Greek philosophical thought had so permeated the intellectual milieu of the Mediterranean world of the Roman Empire that it was perfectly natural for those leaders of the fourth-century church to use the worldview that they had inherited through Greek culture for defining terms such as *son of God* and *Christ* that arose in the culturally different world of ancient Israel and early Judaism. *The way that Christians came to define and understand Jesus in his relation to God was shaped by the language and hence by the culture of the Hellenistic world.* Christianity would have developed very differently had it matured in some culture other than the Hellenism of the Roman Empire.[3]

---

3. There was, of course, a transition into Greek modes of thinking very early in the rise of Christianity. There were Hellenistic influences present in Judea even at the time of Jesus. The author of John's Gospel himself draws on Hellenistic thought patterns as he describes Jesus as the "Word" of God in the opening to his gospel. My point is that these concepts present in Hellenistic thought really shape the way Christianity develops as it moves far-

In fact, one *can* see different ways Christianity develops in different cultural settings. The basic differences between Eastern Christianity in its various Eastern and Russian orthodox forms, and Western Christianity, in its Roman Catholic and Protestant forms, are surely shaped by cultural differences with long histories. More recently, differences between the forms of liturgy and practices in African American churches and those of various European American groups show how different subcultures affect the very presentation and understanding of the Christian gospel. All of this is explained by the notion that historicity is a fundamental characteristic of our human adventure: to be human is to be human in a particular place and a particular time. To understand people in a different place and a different time involves a leap of our imaginations to envision the world through a different set of categories and expectations. A good historian is, to a degree, able to transcend his or her own cultural world to step back into a different world.

But this means that the historical task always involves grounding one's historical interpretation of the past on as much information as possible from the period and place that one studies and then imaginatively reconstructing that situation. That we can transcend our own cultural worldview and enter into the worldviews of others is precisely what makes us aware of our historicity. If we weren't able to transcend our limitations, then we would not be aware of the ways that different cultures shape our views and experiences of the world. Otherwise we'd see our view of the world as *the* world and attribute others' views to ignorance or error. Regrettably, there are those today who cannot transcend their cultural world and mistakenly take it to be the world as it really is in itself.

The recognition of our historicity and the limitations it imposes upon us can lead to a disabling relativity. If indeed our

---

ther away from its original roots in the movement begun by a Galilean Jew in early first-century Palestine. For the story of the Council of Nicea, see Pelikan 1971–89, 1:172-225.

thought and experience are shaped by our cultures, then we can never know Truth as it is in itself. Some would take this as reason to adopt a form of relativism that holds there is no objective world apart from our cultures and no truth, only our prejudices and politically motivated inclinations which masquerade as objectivity. I will address this development more explicitly in chapter 3, in which we explore the impact of pluralism and multiculturalism on our thinking. But I do want to say a few words here about this view that historicism necessarily results in a nihilistic relativism that denies that we can know truth.

To say that we see the world only as that world is shaped by the tools embedded in our culture's language and thought patterns is not to say that there is no reality outside our thinking, which in turn shapes and limits it. Too often the issue is posed in terms of a dichotomy between absolutism and relativism: either what we know is simply a reflection of the reality out there or there is no reality out there and it's all in our heads. I reject this as a false dichotomy. It is intellectually appealing to find a position that is unambiguous and clear, but in this case, neither of the two alternatives is satisfactory. Why? Because the world as we experience it is multidimensional. There are concrete, physical elements to it that are the objects of our sensory perceptions, but then there are many other dimensions, for example, moral, spiritual, and aesthetic ones, which are not simply the passive product of our sensory perceptions. Our human world is not the world of physical objects alone; it is the world of our experience, much of which cannot be understood solely on the basis of immediate sensory perceptions.

Take, for instance, the human trait of acting toward goals and ends. I have in mind as I write this chapter, the way that it will fit into the completed book of which it will be a part. The whole book at the point in time at which I'm writing this sentence is far from complete. But what has already been written at this point only exists because I can envision the rest of the argument in my head. I can imaginatively envision the publication of this book, and that enables me to do the hours upon hours of work necessary to write the individual sentences, paragraphs, and chapters that are the means to achieve the completed project.

One could think of many other examples of this facet of our humanness because the ability to act toward unrealized goals is another fundamental characteristic of our life. Because we can imagine the future, we are not limited to our immediate sensory experience. Because I can imagine the benefits of being in better aerobic condition, I can even continue my exercise program in spite of the sensory discomfort that it sometimes immediately brings. But, on the other hand, I would be foolish to deny the crucial role that the physical world plays in achieving my desire for aerobic conditioning. There are, after all, the hills I climb on my bicycle, which cause physical muscles to burn oxygen, which in turn increases my heart rate and blood flow. To say that important components of human life are not reducible to physical explanation is not to deny the important role physical reality plays in experience.

Most of our experience falls between the poles of external physical reality and our imagination's appropriation of our culture's sets of signs and meanings. But various aspects of our experience fall at different places along the continuum between the poles. In the disciplines of the natural sciences, our thinking and experience tend to be more determined by immediate physical reality; whereas, in disciplines such as aesthetics and ethics, the inherited cultural signs and meanings hold more sway.

When any discipline takes its particular model for truth as the paradigm for all disciplines, then we enter into fruitless debates in which we listen but fail to hear each other. Natural scientists accuse the humanities and social sciences of being fuzzy disciplines because they can't reach the same level of agreement in their disciplines as scientists can achieve in theirs. Humanists and social scientists accuse natural scientists of failing to see that science itself is a social construct that arises out of power struggles between the elite and the masses. To recognize that all of our experience is shaped by both physical reality and the spiritual reality conveyed in our culture, is to see that different aspects of human experience need to be studied with different tools and that the criteria for truth that are applicable in one area may not be the same criteria that are applicable in another.

Historicism is precisely this same recognition taken historically and cross-culturally. To understand another's experience means we must situate ourselves in their place and time as much as this is possible. Like the dichotomy between physical reality and cultural reality, the dichotomy between either having a single common human experience or having no understanding beyond our own time and place is a false choice. Acknowledging that others live in different cultural worlds is not to deny that we can ever understand them but to recognize that we must work hard to walk empathetically in their shoes, *as much as this is possible,* to see how the world looked to them. It is this recognition of the historicity of human life and thought that has come to define a central moment in our thought today that sets it apart from the thought of our ancestors.

CHAPTER TWO

SCIENCE AND OUR NEW WORLDVIEW

*O*ver the past two centuries, natural science has changed not only the way we live but also the way we see ourselves and the world. The obvious technological advances around us are but the tip of an iceberg. My great-grandfather, a physician in Denton County, Texas, only a hundred years ago rode a horse and buggy to visit his patients on the farms of North Texas where he performed minor surgery on their kitchen tables. There were no cars, no airplanes, no radio, no television, and no computers. The advances in technology during the twentieth century are greater than the cumulative technological advances since at least the time of Christ.

But far more significant intellectually are the theoretical advances in basic science that underlie the technological ones. We understand the world in fundamentally different ways than did our ancestors, especially our early ancestors in Christian faith. Our very acceptance and use of technology presuppose these changes in our scientific understanding. It was this fact that led the New Testament theologian Rudolf Bultmann to say in 1941, "We cannot use electric lights and radios and, in the event of illness, avail ourselves of modern medical and clinical means and at the same time believe in the spirit and wonder world of the New Testament" (Bultmann 1984, 4).

What are the principal changes in our ways of thinking

brought about by natural science and how do they affect our thinking as Christians? I want to look at three great intellectual revolutions in science that have shaped our understanding of the world today: the displacement of human beings from the center of the universe brought about by the recognition that the earth is not at its center; the recognition that the heavens are not qualitatively distinct from our experienced reality but operate under the very same laws of physics that describe falling apples and spinning tops; and the discovery that the whole universe and all creatures on our planet are in process of continuing change and transformation. As a result of these intellectual revolutions, we understand our world very differently from our Christian forebears.

THE DISPLACEMENT OF EARTH AS THE CENTER OF THE UNIVERSE

Early Christianity grew up in a Hellenistic world in which Platonic thinking held intellectual sway. Plato (c. 428-348 B.C.E.) thought that the physical world we experience through our senses is but a shadow of the real world, which was the world of ideas. In fact, he and his followers held that true reality could only be apprehended by the intellect uncorrupted by our senses. The physical and sensory were lesser kinds of reality than the intellectual and the spiritual. The divine stood far removed from the physical world and was associated with the realm of ideas.

Plato's own speculations of the physical structure of the universe are only sketchily described in his extant dialogues (see *Timaeus*, 38b-39c, and the *Republic*, 616c-617d). His associate in the academy, Eudoxus of Cnidus, devised a far more detailed view of the universe as comprising concentric spheres. Aristotle (384–322 B.C.E.) expanded Eudoxus's view and argued that fifty-six such concentric spheres, with the earth at the center and the sphere of the fixed stars at the exterior, were required to explain the motions seen in the heavens (Lloyd 1970, 93). The objects, called planets, which moved against the background of the fixed stars, were embedded in different spheres. The motions of these planets could be explained by the different motions of these nested spheres turning on different axes. Centuries later, the Alexandrian mathematician and astronomer Ptolemy (second century C.E.) fine-tuned Aristotle's celestial spheres into a cosmological system that reigned for centuries as our Western view of the structure of the universe.

In the Middle Ages this Ptolemaic cosmology was combined with religious speculations to produce a comprehensive picture of the universe. There were several important components of this medieval understanding. First, it was fundamentally hierarchical: the outer spheres were higher forms of being than the lower spheres. In the lower spheres, the ones under the lunar sphere, the four elements that constitute material reality were dominant: earth, air, fire, and water. Above the lunar sphere were the various celestial spheres of the visible heavens. Next came the spheres in which the angels dwelt. Finally, the outermost sphere was a sphere that moved the other spheres but did not itself move. This was the dwelling place of God.

Second, the celestial spheres were understood to operate under entirely different powers and influences from those of the lower spheres. In the heavenly spheres, circular motion was the norm, conceived to be the most perfect form of motion. In the lower spheres, linear motion was the norm. Indeed, the heavens were believed to operate under very different influences from those operating in the sublunar spheres.

Third, though the heavenly spheres moved—except for the outermost immobile sphere—they did not change. Indeed, it was held that corruption, decay, growth, and the like were limited to the lower spheres. The visible and invisible heavens were changeless and had, since creation, remained the same.[1]

This way of seeing the universe began to crumble in the sixteenth and seventeenth centuries. The first chisel blows were struck by Nicolaus Copernicus (1473–1543). Copernicus, a

---

1. An excellent summary of this medieval understanding can be found in Grant 1978.

Polish astronomer and minor church official, came up with a simpler way of calculating the movements of the planets. Under the Aristotelian-Ptolemaic system, calculating a planet's retrograde motion—a phenomenon wherein a planet appears to loop back briefly upon its normal easterly course across the background stars—required adding small spheres, called epicycles, rotating on an axis on the surface of the planetary sphere itself. By the fifteenth century a very complex set of spheres and epicycles was required to calculate accurately the observed movements of the planets. Copernicus suggested that simpler calculations could be made if the Sun were positioned in the center of the spherical system and if Earth were considered as one of the planetary spheres. Recognizing that the church held the Aristotelian-Ptolemaic view as part of its teachings, Copernicus waited many years before publishing his calculations, and when he did so he was careful to emphasize that the assumption of the Sun's existing at the center of the universe was merely for the convenience of calculation and not to be taken as descriptively true.

Copernicus's heliocentric model of the universe was not widely accepted until his theoretical assumptions were confirmed by astronomical observations made by Galileo Galilei (1564–1642). Galileo perfected the then-recently invented telescope, which enabled him to observe details of the heavens that no one before had seen. He observed, for instance, that the Moon's surface is pitted with craters and that Jupiter has moons. The earlier cosmology held that the spheres of the heavens were constituted of a different substance that set them totally apart from earthly reality. But in finding uneven craters on the Moon, phases in Venus's appearance, and changes in the size and brightness of Mars, Galileo realized that at least some of the heavenly spheres were not as perfect as had been supposed. His observations led him to advocate Copernican heliocentrism not only as a helpful model for calculating planetary motions but also as an alternative description of the actual structure of the universe. His advocacy for heliocentrism led to his conflict with the authorities of the Roman Catholic Church.

The details of Galileo's troubles with the church are not our central concern, nor are the astronomical details of his discoveries.[2] But a great transformation in our view of the universe began with Copernicus and his staunch advocate Galileo. In the hierarchical universe of the medieval world the earth was at its very center. Granted, in that cosmology the earth was lesser in being and value than the heavenly spheres that encompassed it. Yet the heavenly spheres shared the same center, and that center was the earth. Moreover, this geocentric cosmology fit well with the Christian doctrine of humankind's being created in the image of God. In the creation narratives of Genesis 1, the crowning achievement of creation and the creature given dominion over it was humankind. Christians came to see the whole universe as existing for their benefit and their sustenance. By shifting the earth from the center of the universe, the heliocentrists disrupted this centuries-old way of thinking in which the centrality of humankind in creation was not only a theological but also an astronomical truth.

SEEING THE HEAVENS AND THE EARTH AS THE SAME PHYSICAL REALITY

A second phase in the transition to our modern conception of the universe is epitomized in Isaac Newton's *Principia Mathematica* of 1687. In this work, Newton set forth his famous laws of motion in which mathematical formulas were used to describe the trajectories and forces of moving objects. What was innovative in his work was that the laws of motion could be used with equal accuracy to describe the trajectory of a projectile fired from a cannon, the forces of a ball rolling down an inclined plane, or the orbits of the various planets in the solar system. He was able to include the motions of the planets by proposing a

---

2. Excellent studies of the conflict can be found in Finocchiaro 1989 and Pedersen 1991.

theory of universal gravitation, described by an inverse square law: objects attract each other by a gravitational force that is proportional to the mass of the objects and the inverse square of their distances from each other. His law of gravitation, along with his laws of motion, for the first time unified the entire cosmos under one simple set of mechanical principles describable by mathematical equations.

His feat was significant in our growing understanding of the universe in two ways. First, by showing that the planets operated under the same laws that governed falling apples and slamming doors, Newton pulled the heavens down to earth. No longer could we think of the heavens as a qualitatively different reality. Hence, the gradations in value that had been attributed to the various spheres of the heavens were undercut. Second, by developing the mathematical physics necessary to describe the orbits of the planets and explain the observed motions of the heavens, he showed how natural laws could explain phenomena that before had often been explained only by divine intervention: God's power was now not so much manifested in God's interventions in the world of nature as by God's rule over nature through natural law. Seeing the wisdom of God in nature became a preoccupation of many naturalists after Newton. By uncovering the laws that underlay creation, thinkers believed that they were discovering the principles on which God had created the world. They saw the world as an intricately designed machine and were especially enamored with the fine adaptations that made plants and animals so well suited to their various environments. Only an intelligent creator of infinite wisdom could so craft the many intricacies of creation.

The most famous presentation of this argument was published in 1802 by the Anglican clergyman and philosopher William Paley (1743–1805). *Natural Theology* was to become one of the most widely read English treatises of the nineteenth century. With painstaking detail, Paley gave numerous examples of how animals are adapted to the environments in which they were created. For example, he examines the eye to show how each of its structures contributes to the overall purpose of seeing, just as the lenses and tube of a telescope are designed for the purpose of enlarging an image. The plan behind a telescope is explained by the design given it by its maker; so the thoughtful person must conclude, argued Paley, that an analogous plan must likewise lie behind the many adaptations of organisms to their environments (Paley 1810–12, 1:20-41).

NATURE BECOMES A DYNAMICALLY CHANGING REALITY

One of Paley's enthusiastic young readers was Charles Darwin (1809–82). As a student at Cambridge, Darwin carefully studied Paley's arguments and was intrigued by Paley's detailed examples of how species are adapted to their environments. The opportunity to study further such adaptations was one of the attractions for Darwin to join the crew of the surveying ship HMS *Beagle* as naturalist when the *Beagle* set sail in 1831 to make its way around the world. He did indeed find many examples. But the journey planted in his mind the seeds of a theory to explain adaptation that went in a very different direction from Paley's.

Darwin mulled over his new explanation of adaptation for many years before finally publishing it in 1859 in his *Origin of Species by Means of Natural Selection*. Darwin proposed that the adaptation of organisms to their environments could be explained by a process he called natural selection. Just as animal breeders select for further breeding, offspring that manifest characteristics the breeders favor, so traits that contribute to an individual's survival and reproduction are selected by nature when the fitter individuals survive and produce more offspring. The pressure for survival in an environment in which organisms are competing for resources leads to succeeding generations better adapted to their environment than were the preceding generations.

The idea that nature might work in a way analogous to the way a breeder works, improving the fitness of strains *within* a species, was not all that controversial. After all, animal husbandry was a well-developed skill in the nineteenth century, and selective breeding had already led to various improvements in animal stocks and crop varieties. But Darwin went further than the suggestion that nature produced new varieties within a species by means of natural selection; he also argued that *species themselves were but varieties on a large scale.* Natural selection, over long periods of time, will gradually produce new species. From this, Darwin postulated that all living organisms descended from at most only a few common ancestors. Darwin's own famous words are worthy of note:

> There is grandeur in this view of life, with its several powers, having been originally breathed by the Creator into a few forms or into one; and that, whilst this planet has gone cycling on according to the fixed law of gravity, from so simple a beginning endless forms most beautiful and most wonderful have been, and are being evolved. (1950, 374)

For all that Newton had done to bring the heavens down to earth by giving mathematical descriptions of motion in the universe, he had not challenged the assumption that the present state of the universe is much the way God originally created it, moving along in cyclical motions but not itself in a process of dynamic change. Darwin challenged this static view of creation with his theory of natural selection. Life, all life, is evolving; humans, along with all other animals and all other plants, are the result of millions of years of evolution. Darwin was not able to explain how variations arose nor the mechanisms by which the variations were passed down to succeeding generations—those problems were not finally solved until the twentieth century. But by the late 1870s, his argument that existing species arose from earlier forms through descent with modification was accepted by a majority of British naturalists (Bowler 1989, 189-99). Today evolution is a fundamental building block of biological science and hence of our modern understanding of human origins.

The organic world as we see it today is dynamic and continually evolving. Because the time frame of our individual lives is so short and even the time frame of human history is short when compared with the overall time involved in the process of organic evolution, we do not see the dynamics of change. In our limited perspective, nature looks stable and unchanging. But it is not. Indeed, the very stars themselves, which our ancestors took to be fixed in the outermost visible celestial sphere, are moving and changing. The discovery of cosmic evolution is one of the great advances of the twentieth century.[3]

In the first half of the twentieth century, new and large optical telescopes of high quality made the observation of distant galaxies possible. Also during this period the technique of spectral analysis of light was developed. Combining these two technological innovations, astronomers discovered an interesting and surprising fact: there was a telltale redshift in the color spectrum of light from distant galaxies. To appreciate the significance of this discovery, we first must examine the properties of light.

Light is a form of electromagnetic radiation. What distinguishes light from other forms of electromagnetic radiation—heat or radio waves, for instance—is its wavelength or frequency: visible light falls in the narrow band of wavelengths between about 4×10^{-7} and 7×10^{-7} meters. We experience the different wavelengths in this band as different colors. White light is light made up of a wide spectrum of wavelengths, or colors. When white light is separated into its different components, we see the light spectrum as a series of differently colored bands. Sunlight is split into its component colors when a rainbow appears in the sky: small water droplets in the atmosphere refract the light into its components. This same phenomenon can be achieved by projecting a beam of light through a prism. The phenomenon was refined into a precise optical instrument called a spectro-

---

3. I am indebted to Weinberg (1988) for much of the information in the following discussion of the "big bang."

scope, which gave precise breakdowns of the various wavelengths of light directed through the instrument.

In the 1920s and 1930s, Edwin Hubble (1889–1953), combining the technological innovations of spectroscopy and the newer, more powerful telescopes, noted that the particular spectral patterns of the light from distant galaxies were shifted to slightly longer wavelengths (toward the red end of the color spectrum) than the patterns obtained by examining the light from nearer stars. Moreover, the shift appeared greater the more distant the galaxy. How was this shift to be explained?

This shift is explained by a phenomenon known as the Doppler effect. We're familiar with this phenomenon as it can be perceived in sound. Like light, sound has properties of physical waves, including different wavelengths and frequencies. When a car honking its horn passes by us we can hear a slight change in its pitch. This change in pitch occurs because, as the sound leaves the horn of an approaching car, the car's movement toward us actually compresses the sound waves and this increases the frequency (pitch) of the sound. As the car moves away from us, the opposite happens: the sound gets lower in pitch. The movement of the car actually increases or decreases the wavelength, thus raising or lowering the pitch. If we had three identically pitched horns, one standing still, one traveling toward us, and one traveling away from us, the two in movement would be perceived as having different pitches, one higher and one lower, than the horn at rest, although in fact they all produce the same sound.

The same phenomenon occurs with light emitted from very rapidly moving objects. We do not perceive such effects in our everyday world: a car's headlight doesn't change color as it passes by us. Yet at the extremely high speeds involved in the movements of stars and galaxies, the change in color can be detected by spectral analysis of the light. Hubble used the Doppler effect to explain the redshift in the color spectra emitted by distant galaxies by suggesting that galaxies were not stationary, as was commonly believed, but must be moving away from us. Just as the pitch of a car's horn that is moving away from us sounds lower, so the light from a receding galaxy looks redder than would be expected from a stationary galaxy. Moreover, the farther away the galaxy, the more pronounced is the redshift in its spectrum: thus, the more distant a galaxy, the faster it must be moving away from us. The very stars that had been the sign of changeless perfection for our ancestors are now known to be ever changing, with the most distant hurtling away from each other at enormous speeds. The distances to these stars and galaxies are so enormous that their movements have been mostly imperceptible over the brief span of recorded history.

Another important piece to this puzzle was found in the 1960s. In 1965 two scientists at Bell Laboratories, Arno Penzias and Robert W. Wilson, were puzzled by data they had collected as they tried to calibrate a new instrument for measuring electromagnetic emissions from the stars at radio wavelengths. In their attempts to set up the instrument they discovered an annoying radio "noise" that appeared no matter where in the sky they pointed the radio antenna. After eliminating the possibility that the instrument itself was the source of the noise, they concluded that there was a very slight but consistent background radiation throughout the universe. What was the source of this radiation? They found the answer when their measurements were combined with the theoretical work of the Princeton physicist P. J. E. Peoples, who had before their discovery theorized that the radiation resulting from the initial formation of the universe should still be measurable. Later work confirmed that the background radiation they had discovered was indeed the remnants of heat originally released in the initial explosion of a primordial fireball and subsequent rapid expansion of the universe—the "big bang" as it popularly came to be called. The reason the galaxies showed a redshift in their spectra was because the universe is rapidly expanding as a result of the big bang that began the universe as we know it. The heavens, rather than being changeless and static, are dynamic and expanding. And we are passengers on Earth, which is part of a solar system, which is part of a galaxy, which is part of this rapidly expanding universe.

The explanatory power of this model of the universe is truly remarkable. Combined with discoveries concerning the origin of the chemical elements in the dynamics of star formation, growth, and collapse, we have today a sketch of the universe that sees the evolution of life as but one piece of the overall process of cosmic evolution. Indeed, we have learned that the chemical elements that compose our bodies were forged in the middle of aging stars and released as a result of those stars' collapsing in upon themselves in stellar explosions called supernovas. Scientists who work in particle physics to study the smallest components of matter have joined up with astrophysicists, who study the large-scale physics of the universe, to produce a theory of the origins of our universe resulting from a single big bang some fifteen billion years ago. Since that point the universe has been in the process of constant change; the process has resulted in the evolution of the galaxies, our own solar system, our own planet, and life upon our planet. Indeed, that process has resulted in the evolution of human beings who are conscious of this grand process that brought us into being and sustains us in being.

The big bang theory is a grand story, but one very different from that told by our ancestors in Christian faith. Relying on the stories of the beginning of the world told by their own ancestors in ancient Israel, Christians in past centuries accepted a very different picture of how creation came to be. Limited by the information available to them and the conceptual worlds of their day and time, they saw the world as crafted by God, much the way a human artisan crafts an object. But those who take seriously the advances in our understanding brought about by the sciences over the past few centuries simply cannot see the origins of the universe in the way that our ancestors did. Our modern scientific understanding of the universe and of the evolution of life on our planet compels us as Christians to rethink our inheritance, to sort through our faith, and to recognize that we need to develop new ways of thinking about God's creative activity in the cosmic evolutionary process. We are created by God to live in this day and time. If, in this day and time, our knowledge of the world suggests we need to rethink some of the ways our ancestors thought about the world, so be it. As I will argue in chapter 4, just such rethinking is required as we read our ancestors' stories of creation in the book of Genesis.

But this rethinking does not require that we jettison along with the ancient cosmology the religious truths that arise from those stories, truths concerning God's creative relation to the world and God's sovereign dominion over it. Yet this, sadly, is the only option that some believers think they have. Each semester I teach an introduction to the Bible. On occasion, a student reports that she has been taught in her church that one either accepts the Bible as literally and historically true in all its passages or one is not a true Christian. Such an approach pits modern scientific understandings against the biblical myths of creation as if they were competing explanatory schemes for the origin of the universe. Indeed, in the past several decades, fundamentalist Christians in the United States have launched a movement to promote teaching the main lines of the biblical story of creation in public schools as an alternative to the modern scientific understanding. The movement, often referred to by its proponents as *scientific creationism* or *creation science,* was actually influential enough in the 1970s and early 1980s that laws were passed in Arkansas and Louisiana requiring that the alternative Genesis-based story of the universe be taught if the modern scientific view of evolution were taught. The federal courts wisely struck down those laws as unconstitutional on the basis of the First Amendment because the laws required states to promote a particular religious view. But the movement is still active at the levels of local school boards and textbook selection committees, and its proponents like to leave the impression that scientists really are divided on whether the universe came about by an evolutionary process or by a miraculous, relatively short creation process driven directly by the intervening action of a creator. *But the vast majority of scientists aren't divided on this issue.* The notion that the universe gradually developed over billions of years and that life on earth arose in that process and evolved through mechanisms involving natural selection is really a settled issue in science. True, not all the details have been worked out and debates rage over particular components of the overall view. But the only scientists who suggest that the book of Genesis contains a "scientific" alternative to cosmic evolution are those who are beforehand committed to a literal inerrantist view of scripture.[4] Other scientists who are committed to Christian faith recognize that in discovering the structures, mechanisms, and processes of the universe's history one is not betraying one's faith in God but living out an aspect of it. After all, if God is the creator of the world and we are committed to the view that the creation is good, then truths about the world are also truths about God and God's being. In this sense we today are not so far from those seventeenth- and eighteenth-century Anglican divines who sought the wisdom of God among the works of creation. We certainly won't find the same things they found because their approach assumed a static creation. But what we find must be viewed through the eyes of faith as being *of and from God.*

Looking back over the history of Christian faith and theology, one thing is clear: nothing was ever gained by Christians' denial of our growing knowledge about the natural world. Far too many examples can be adduced—from the church's accusations of heresy against Galileo to the fundamentalist attacks on evolution in the famous Scopes monkey trial—that show how fruitless it is to deny new discoveries about our natural world and how risky it is to present Christian faith in such a way that one

---

4. This fact was pointed out by Judge Overton in his District Court decision invalidating the Arkansas law requiring creation science to be taught in the public schools if evolution were taught. He noted that membership in the "research" organization promoting creation science, the Creation Research Society, required as a condition of membership that a scientist sign a pledge of belief in the Genesis account as being historically and scientifically true (*McLean v. Arkansas Bd. of Ed.* 529 F. Supp. 1255 [1982]).

must give up one's intellect to believe in God. But a re-visioned Christian faith, taking account of our contemporary knowledge of the natural world as well as of our new understandings of history and historical development, is not only possible but necessary if the gospel is to remain alive as a viable witness to faith in God in the twenty-first century. Outlining such a re-visioned faith will be the central concern of the second half of this book. But one more stop is necessary in our characterization of the state of contemporary thinking in the academy before we attempt to re-vision Christian faith, and that is the discussions of multiculturalism and pluralism that shape intellectual debate today.

CHAPTER THREE

LISTENING TO OTHER VOICES

*T*he rise of scientific methods to explore our physical world and the rise of critical-historical methods to examine our historical world are two great achievements of Western thought. To live in the Western world at the turn of the twenty-first century is to be shaped by these intellectual revolutions, whether we're conscious of their influence or not. To read newspaper accounts of crimes or airline crashes, to go to the polls to approve bond issues for new water treatment plants or supercolliding superconductors, to take medicines prescribed by our physicians—all depend on the basic assumptions of modern scientific and historical knowledge.

AUTHORITY AND THE RISE OF THE AUTONOMOUS SELF

We must remember, however, that prior to these revolutions our intellectual ancestors lived their lives under very different assumptions, both implicit and explicit. Their thought was heavily determined by appeals to authorities. In the medieval world, these authorities in the universities were first and foremost the written authorities of the past. Much of the scholarship in the medieval world was in the form of commentaries on the great texts of the past. Peter Lombard's *Books of Sentences* (1148–51) was a standard theological text in the medieval world; it was a collection of excerpts from the early church fathers and com-

49

mentaries on those excerpts. Even medieval medicine proceeded on the basis of the authority of texts. The almost thousand-year-old works of the second-century Greek physician Galen were the standard texts on which medical training was based. It's difficult for us, who live on the other side of the scientific revolution, even to conceive that anyone should think that the best way to learn anatomy is by reading a centuries-old text rather than by carefully dissecting cadavers. But our difficulty of conceiving the medieval approach to knowledge simply demonstrates the very thesis for which I'm arguing: today we see things very differently from our ancestors because we live with very different understandings of the world, ourselves, and our place in the world.

The period known as the Renaissance began to break from the patterns of the Middle Ages, but it did so by returning to the ancient world of classical Greece and Rome as the locus of authoritative texts. The beginnings of our modern ways of thinking are best traced to the period known as the Enlightenment, generally understood as culminating in the eighteenth century. Here a break with the older approaches to knowledge based on authorities was decisively made. Immanuel Kant (1724–1804) best sums up this new attitude in an essay he published in 1784 entitled "What is Enlightenment?":

> Enlightenment is man's release from his self-incurred tutelage. Tutelage is man's inability to make use of his understanding without direction from another. Self-incurred is this tutelage when its cause lies not in lack of reason but in lack of resolution and courage to use it without direction from another. *Sapere aude!* [Dare to know!] "Have courage to use your own reason!"— that is the motto of the Enlightenment. (1957, 3)

The phrase "without direction from another" well sums up the Enlightenment's confidence in the autonomous self's ability to discover truth.

The optimistic and progressive confidence in the autonomous self to discover all truth using the methods of natural science has come under serious challenge in recent decades. In the humanities and social sciences this modern Enlightenment notion of truth has been rigorously attacked from several flanks. To understand fully the *postmodernist* challenge to Enlightenment modernity, however, we must turn to the father of modernity himself, René Descartes (1596–1650). His ideas became the foundation stones on which all of modern thought was built.

DESCARTES AND THE PROJECT OF MODERNITY

Descartes set out to change the very directions of European culture. The idea that one pursued truth through reading and accepting authorities worked as long as the culture of Europe had an agreed upon set of authorities. Western Europe had a single church for centuries of its history; this certainly contributed to the fundamental agreements over the appropriate authorities. But after the singular hold that the Roman Catholic Church had on Europe was broken in the sixteenth century by the Protestant Reformation, the issue of authority became a matter of disagreement. With the rise of the Lutheran and Reformed churches, European princes had to choose between loyalty to the Roman Catholic Church or to one of the new Protestant movements. Wars broke out among German princes as a result of this new religious pluralism. The Thirty Years' War embroiled Europe in hostilities from 1618 until 1648 as a result of the loss of a singular religious and political authority in Europe.

Most of Descartes's adult life was spent under the shadow of the Thirty Years' War. Descartes wanted to find some solid basis for knowledge that would break from the tradition of appeals to authority, appeals which seemed fruitless in the face of the conflicting authorities that were the genesis of the wars. In this situation, Descartes turned to the self and its reasoning abilities as the new authority.[1]

---

1. See Toulmin 1990 for an insightful discussion of Descartes's work in light of the Thirty Years' War.

Descartes retreated entirely from the resources of knowledge then available and went deep within his own thought to find a sure and certain foundation for truth. In his *Discourse on Method* he describes the occasion when, during the above-mentioned wars he spent a day "shut up in a room heated by an enclosed stove" (1968, 27). Totally isolated from all outside influences and utterly alone, he explores the foundations of his knowledge by attempting to doubt everything he thinks he knows, by this means hoping to find something sure and certain on which he might rebuild all his knowledge. What he discovers is that he cannot doubt that *he* is doubting. In trying to doubt that he exists he must at least assume that there is a *he* who doubts. Think about this sentence: "I don't exist." It is a sentence that contradicts itself, for the predicate denies the subject. Speaking the sentence, however, affirms the existence of the *I* who is the subject of the sentence. Hence it is impossible to doubt one's own existence. Descartes believed that in this discovery he had found the one certain and indubitable truth claim on which to build all other knowledge. Ultimately it is the self, autonomous and alone, that must reconstruct truth based on the self's own authority. The modern turn from external authorities to the internal authority of the self had begun.

POSTMODERNIST CHALLENGES TO MODERNITY

University of Chicago theologian David Tracy, whose recent works have explored the collapse of modernity and the rise of postmodern thinking, summarizes the achievements of Descartes's project (1987; 1994). Modernity accepted and is defined by four important points in Descartes's new approach: "the drive to clarity, the turn to the subject, the concern with method, [and] the belief in sameness" (Tracy 1994, 104). I'll briefly comment on the first three points before we turn the rest of our attention to the issue of sameness.

The drive to clarity in modern thought has typically involved finding certain indubitable propositions on which all thinkers can agree. In Descartes's rationalistic approach to certainty this involved the discovery of those propositions that all rational thinkers would find clear and distinct. All other true knowledge would be deduced from these basic clear and distinct ideas. To determine if something is true, one must analyze the claim into its constituent components and show how these components come to rest in the clear and distinct ideas that are the presuppositions of the whole system.

Later, empiricism would refine Descartes's approach. Whereas Descartes held that many of the most basic clear and distinct ideas were innate to us, lying within our minds and needing only reawakening, the empiricists—and I have especially in mind the father and epitome of empiricism, John Locke—held that all our ideas are founded on either our sensory experience or our experience of reflecting on the operations of our mind (Locke 1975, 104-6). At birth our minds are blank tablets, which experience begins to fill in from its two sources. Thus, although Descartes and Locke see very different origins for our clear and distinct ideas, they both agree that knowledge must be built up from a foundation of such ideas.

This modern notion that knowledge must be based on certain and indubitable foundations has come under attack in philosophy. Indeed, for many postmodern critics, it is precisely the foundationalism of the modernist project that is centrally suspect. Philosophers as diverse as Alvin Plantinga (1983), a conservative Christian, and Richard Rorty (1979), a skeptical relativist, have assaulted this notion that only knowledge resting on indubitable foundations is valid. A second criticism comes into play here: the modernist project, say its critics, was too concerned with developing a universal method, modeled on the methods successful in the natural sciences, which emphasized founding truth claims on empirical, sensory experiences that all human beings can potentially share. This is reflected in the scientific method's emphasis on repeatability: if an experiment cannot be reproduced by another scientist—potentially *any* qualified scientist—then the observations of the original experimenter must be judged as erroneous or insufficient.

By the 1920s the drive toward certainty and scientific methodology led to a movement in philosophy known as *logical positivism*. The positivists hoped to solve all of philosophy's persistent questions by adopting a mathematically and scientifically based approach. The positivists held that for a question to have any meaning it must be statable in terms that can be scientifically verified. Hence, by stipulation, the logical positivists banished many of what had been central philosophical problems to the realm of meaningless assertions. Ethics and theology were treated in this way, as well as questions of aesthetics. But logical positivism was hoisted by its own petard when its opponents made the forceful case that the very principle on which the whole of positivism was built—the notion that meaningful assertions were to be limited to assertions that could be empirically verified—was itself not empirically verifiable. Hence, logical positivism was founded on a principle that was, on the positivists' own definition, meaningless.[2]

What of the "turn to the subject" about which Tracy speaks? Modernity was built on the fundamental assumption of the autonomy of the individual self. The challenge of the Enlightenment, as we've seen in the above citation from Kant, was for each individual to "dare to know." Each individual now became an autonomous center whose value was not to be judged in light of some hierarchical social or metaphysical structure. Moreover, each individual was called to take responsibility for himself (the masculine pronoun is used here intentionally, for the Enlightenment understood its claims as primarily applying to men and not women), his beliefs, and his actions. This principle of autonomy is as well the foundation of liberal democracy, so well illustrated in the founding documents of the United States. "We hold these

---

2. A classic statement of the positivists' position can be found in Ayer 1952. A good summary of the criticisms of positivism can be found in Passmore 1967.

truths to be self-evident," in the words of the Declaration of Independence, "that all Men are created equal, that they are endowed by their Creator with certain inalienable Rights, that among these are Life, Liberty, and the Pursuit of Happiness." Each individual has rights directly endowed by the Creator, so that each subject is equal in his relationships with others. This profoundly modern notion becomes the foundational assumption of our democratic understanding of rights and liberties.

And this well illustrates the ambiguity attached to modernity's legacy: on the one hand, defining and promulgating liberal democracy is one of the greatest achievements of the West; on the other, modernity seems to have reached a dead end in its attempt to find the universal certainties on which to base all truth and value. It is modernity's assumption of sameness that is most under challenge today by postmodernity's emphasis on otherness.

Modernity's appeal to a common human reason exercised in the context of common starting points and assumptions was part and parcel of the Enlightenment project. As Tracy notes, it resulted in a concern with method. Indeed, the very notion first proposed by Descartes, that a common method could be applied to diverse fields of inquiry, deeply influenced all subsequent thought. In the natural sciences, the assumption of a single methodology leading to a single set of descriptive laws and principles has found much success. But when studying human cultures and belief systems, the assumption of commonality has led to serious deficiencies. Only in recent decades have we become fully aware that what our forebears took to be a common human reason and common human values were really quite culturally specific and temporally bound. Postmodern thinking has taught us the irreducible realities of otherness.

Many of us have personally experienced this growing awareness of otherness. I remember as a young boy believing that Christianity was the true religion of humankind. If it were the true religion, then other religions were either mistaken in their understandings of ultimate reality or were trying to express the same thing as Christianity but in different words. I thought other religions were not genuinely alternative visions of reality; they were the result of ignorance. What we in the church needed to do was simple: I thought we could all become one by teaching Christianity to others across the world and, having seen the true light in the process, those others would become like us. A similar naiveté underlay my view of the civil rights movement in the 1950s and 1960s. I was deeply committed to desegregation and the integration of the races. But my vision was one in which blacks and Hispanics would lose their otherness and become like middle-class white Americans. I believed that we were all one (which I still believe) and hence we ought all to be the same (which I now do not believe). The particular postmodern problem is how we recognize difference, genuine otherness, as a fundamental characteristic of our humanity without always trying to fit that otherness into a scheme or pattern that finally fails to take it seriously as genuinely other but instead sees it either as an underdeveloped form of our own view or as a mistake.

FEMINIST THOUGHT AND OTHERNESS

The significance of otherness in postmodern thought confronts our thinking about Christian faith in many areas. I want to examine two areas: feminism and the world's religions. Women have, of course, been around since the very beginnings of human life and culture! Indeed, sexual differentiation appeared as a reproductive strategy early in the evolution of life. Our own biblical tradition is full of stories involving women. Women even constitute a majority of church members in the United States. How can we say, then, that feminism needs to be taken more seriously in our postmodern context? Haven't women always been taken seriously in our culture and religious tradition?

What feminist thought has called to our attention is just what it really means for women to be taken seriously. Feminist thinkers have pointed to the patriarchal character of European culture generally and of Christianity more specifically. Patriarchy, as defined by the feminist historian Gerda Lerner,

> means the manifestation and institutionalization of male dominance over women and children in the family and the extension of male dominance over women in society in general. It implies that men hold power in all the important institutions of society and that women are deprived of access to such power. It does *not* imply that women are either totally powerless or totally deprived of rights, influence, and resources. (1986, 239)

In a patriarchal system, women are taken seriously when they conform to the roles expected of them by the male-defined and male-dominated system. But the question that feminist thinkers ask today is whether those roles defined by patriarchy don't need reexamination. For feminist thinkers, taking women seriously means seeing women's experience as equally definitive as men's experience of what it means to be human, which in far too many cases has been simply accepted as definitive of human experience in general.

Feminism is a basic challenge to the modern notion that human experience is the same for all persons. By showing the ways that men's experience has been accepted in our past as definitive of all human experience and by showing the unique contributions women's experience can make to our understanding of human being, feminists have raised our consciousness about the implicit and often deeply buried assumptions and presuppositions of our societies and our religions.

Likewise, feminist theologians working within the traditions of Christianity have significantly raised our consciousness as Christians about the implicit and deeply buried presuppositions and prejudices that we have inherited from our forebears. The religions of ancient Israel and of early Christianity were born in cultures that were patriarchal in character. As these religions developed they conformed to the social structures of those patriarchal worlds. And yet embedded within them are also stories that suggest women played important roles; but these women are hidden by the way the stories are passed on in the tradition. Elisabeth Schüssler Fiorenza reminds us of one of these women. We find her in Mark 14 and its parallels in Matthew 26 and Luke 7. This unnamed woman anoints Jesus with costly oil, causing his disciples to chastise her for wasting the money. But Jesus replies to them, "Truly I tell you, wherever the good news is proclaimed in the whole world, what she has done will be told in remembrance of her" (Mark 14:9). Schüssler Fiorenza poignantly asks if this woman's deed *is* recounted wherever the good news is proclaimed. No, the deed we remember from this chapter in Mark is rather the deed of Judas Iscariot, who betrayed Jesus (Schüssler Fiorenza 1983, xii–xiv). It is a woman who anoints Jesus, the act symbolizing kingship in Israel; this suggests that women played a larger role among Jesus' early followers than later preservers of the Jesus tradition were wont to convey.

The forgotten role of women in the early Jesus movement is something that can be recovered, to a degree, by historical research and social analysis of the world in which Christianity spread. But no amount of historical digging will overcome the fact that Jesus talked of God as "Father," and his early followers soon came to speak of Jesus as God's son. The very root symbols with which Christians have over the centuries spoken of God and Jesus are masculine. For some feminists, these symbols are too entwined in patriarchy to serve anymore as symbols of the divine. These post-Christian feminists have turned from Christianity, some to develop specifically feminist approaches to spirituality.[3] But many feminists remain strongly committed to Christianity and the basic symbols of faith.

One such Christian feminist is Elizabeth A. Johnson. In *She Who Is: The Mystery of God in Feminist Theological Discourse* (1994), Johnson argues that Christianity's message of liberation and divine compassion transcend the particular male symbols in

---

3. See, for example, Daly 1984.

which this message was first expressed. Indeed, she thinks the very notion of the Trinity incorporates mutuality and equality within the divine, characteristics that feminist thinkers value highly in women's experience. She also argues that if we really understand the classical doctrine of the full humanity of Jesus, we will see that it refers to Jesus' *humanity* not his masculinity, though many in the church have subtly collapsed these two categories into one. Recognizing that "ideas of God are cultural creatures related to the time and place in which they are conceived" (1994, 273), she goes on to propose the need for Christians to plumb the depths of our own tradition to find the feminine symbols buried therein and to develop new symbols to talk more adequately about God in our day and time, symbols that include God as mother and as friend. Drawing on the Gospel of John's clear allusion to the image of Woman Wisdom found in the book of Proverbs, who is described as being brought forth at the beginning of creation and working with God "beside him" (Proverbs 8:22-31), Johnson suggests that additional symbols for God are appropriate today, including the image of God as *sophia*, the Greek word for wisdom.

Feminist thought has deeply influenced contemporary Christian theology. But the serious engagement of women in our culture more generally—through the workforce, through the political process, through the intellectual worlds—has deeply affected the way we view women today. I think few today, even among the most ardent conservatives, would argue that women shouldn't be able to vote in local, state, and national elections. Yet my own grandmothers were unable to vote when they turned twenty-one years old because the Nineteenth Amendment had not yet been ratified. This new consciousness of women has exploded within the twentieth century and changed the way we think about our humanity. It has undoubtedly also influenced the ways we worship and think about God. We'll come back to this latter point in chapter 6 to think through just how feminist thinking calls us to reevaluate some of the images and symbols of God that we have inherited from our Christian forebears. We need now, however, to turn to the second area in which post-modernist thinking confronts our modernist assumption of sameness: the question of otherness embedded in the world's religious traditions.

We live in a global village. Advances in communications technology make possible virtually instantaneous contact across the world for anyone with a telephone or a computer modem. As a result of satellite technology, live feeds from any part of the world can bring live television images of world events into our homes—quite a change from two hundred years ago when a word from another part of the world might take months to arrive! To these advances in communications we must add the improvements made in our modes of transportation that have enabled individuals to move easily from one culture to another. As a result of all these changes, our global economy is rapidly affected by happenings in every part of the world. All of this has made other cultures less alien, less mysterious, and less foreboding.

Technology has also brought about the recognition that we are part of a single ecosystem in which issues of pollution and environmental abuse ramify across the globe. The damage done to the upper atmosphere by the use of chlorofluorocarbons, especially the use of refrigerants by the industrialized West, affects even the most isolated peoples on our Earth. The massive clearing of the rain forests in South America, for the purpose of claiming arable lands for agriculture, may have catastrophic effects on our planet's oxygen levels since the rain forests are an important producer of Earth's supply of oxygen.

And, of course, we've not even spoken of the unspeakable: the ability that several nations now have to unleash massive nuclear war, the results of which could be as devastating to our planet's ecosystem as the last great impact Earth suffered from a comet, which many scientists now believe brought about the extinction of many forms of life, including the dinosaurs. For our forebears, wars were usually localized and limited in their effects. But as civilizations have advanced, so have the technologies of war. A war between two small nations that have nuclear capability, though they may be on the other side of the world from us, is a war that potentially has serious impact on us through radioactive fallout. We're all tied together today in an immense global village in which the actions of even our distant neighbors directly affect us.

But unlike the simpler villages of traditional societies, the global village we now confront remains extremely pluralistic and diverse. Things that were the strongest unifiers in traditional cultures, like common history, common language, and common religion, are precisely the things that diverge the most in our global world. Thus, technology has brought us into the situation of a global village, but the things that unify traditional villages are absent.

Part of the Enlightenment's quest for sameness was the hope that a single religion could absorb the many religions of the world. For some, this was a hope that Christianity could be shown to be the most advanced and, hence, the best expression of the world's religions. Friedrich Schleiermacher's *On Religion: Speeches to Its Cultured Despisers*, written in 1799, argues this way. At the turn of the nineteenth century, his proposal to treat all the world's religions as variants of the same basic human phenomenon was revolutionary. Christians weren't used to thinking of Islam and Buddhism as having anything in common with Christianity. They had always assumed that the relation between Christianity and the other religions was not one of cousins but of mortal enemies. Schleiermacher, however, suggested that all religions were to be understood as the expressions in different cultures of a fundamental *feeling of absolute dependence*, a feeling that all humans have deep within them. Christianity, he went on to argue, is the best expression of this feeling and hence is the highest form of religion. But other religions are not to be so quickly dismissed as heresy, since they are but differing, less mature expressions of the same fundamental feeling that is expressed in Christianity (Schleiermacher 1963).

Others in the Enlightenment were not so quick to celebrate Christianity as the one religion that could encompass all the others. The new confidence in human reason, which was the foundation of Descartes's whole way of thinking, led some to attempt to develop a religion based on human reason alone. There had always been, in Christian thinking, the idea that people could know something of God by the use of reason apart from revelation. But this knowledge of God derived from reason was always taken to be insufficient for salvation. Modernity's new confidence in reason, however, led many to propose that religion itself needed to heed the new methods and procedures of Enlightenment thinking and to drop the dependence on revelation, which was seen as the last vestige of dependence on authority that kept people in servitude and bondage. The many forms of *deism* that arose in the eighteenth century were attempts to rely on reason alone for religious knowledge. Several of our own founding fathers, especially Thomas Jefferson, author of the Declaration of Independence, were heavily influenced by this religion of reason. But attempts to advocate a religion of reason apart from the historical religious traditions failed.

They failed, we now realize, because humans are not simply reasoning beings. They are always reasoning beings *within* a cultural and historical context. Indeed, this is one of the fundamental characteristics of human beings that modernity simply failed to take with full seriousness. The very way we see and envision divine reality is contingent on the categories, myths, and symbols that are available to us. We can't step back fully from those categories, myths, and symbols to see how divine reality *really* is, because divine reality is mediated to us *through* these things.

So what are we left with? We're left with many religions in our global village. Indeed, today we work alongside of and live next door to persons who live out of other faith traditions. Our growing awareness of those traditions, both in popular culture and in the academic study of religion, has led us to take those of other faiths more seriously. As we get to know adherents of other religions and study their worldviews, we begin to realize the profound depth and seriousness of those traditions. And knowing these others affects the way we see our own religion and our own beliefs.

Postmodernity takes seriously the presence of the other. And taking seriously the other in other world religions will mean that we must think of our own tradition in new ways. Early Christianity became a missionary faith, competing with other faiths in the Roman world. It evolved rapidly into an exclusive message of salvation. But because we live in a global village, because we now see that our religious traditions arise in particular cultures that come to influence the categories, myths, and symbols that describe and invoke those traditions, and because we've come to know persons of other traditions and have come to appreciate the depth and structure of those other traditions' articulations of the divine—because of all these things we must think about our faith in new ways, rethink some of the basic categories that we've inherited, and be willing to reconstruct the myths and symbols that express and constitute our faith in God. That is the task we'll turn to in the second part of this book as we ask how we can think about our Christian faith today in ways that take seriously what we at the end of the twentieth century have come to know about ourselves and our world.

PART
TWO

RETHINKING

CHRISTIAN

FAITH

CHAPTER FOUR

THINKING ABOUT THE BIBLE TODAY

I've argued in the foregoing chapters that we must, as Christians, take seriously the discoveries about our world and how we think about ourselves in the world which have been the legacy of the past two centuries. Our understanding of nature, of the past, and of the diversity within human culture leads us to experience life differently from our forebears. *We do not see the same world they saw.* As tempting as it might be to return to the security and tranquillity of the good old days, we cannot. Even to bring into the present the values adhered to in the past is to transform those values into present ones.

The Bible is central to our faith as Christians. From the most conservative biblical inerrantist to the most liberal social activist, Christians hold this book as special for the life of faith. But how is it special? Forebears in our tradition have called the Bible the inspired Word of God and Divine Revelation. But how can we view this book in light of current knowledge? Some Christians think it can be pulled from its historical past directly into the present. But others of us think this impossible, given what we know about the Bible's origins and history. If we take seriously the developments in modern and postmodern thought, how can we view the Bible today?

The Bible is our foundational document as Christians. It gives witness to the origins of the religious tradition out of which we come and in which we live. It has been revered through the centuries, translated more than any other book, and still stands as a perennial best-seller. Moreover, no other book has had a greater influence on the development of Western culture. It continues to be widely read and influential.

Yet we can't read the Bible as our ancestors in faith read the Bible. What we've learned over the past two hundred years about the Bible, its historical context, and the nature of ancient literature prevents our reading the Bible as our great-grandparents and grandparents read it. And what we've learned in science about the natural world and in history about our social and political pasts, too, precludes our approaching the Bible as earlier Christians approached it.

The single most important development for understanding our relation to the Bible today is *biblical criticism*. Scholars use the term *criticism* in its fullest sense, not the narrow sense it has in popular use where *critical* usually means something negative. In the fullest sense, to be critical is to make a judgment or evaluation that may be positive or negative. In popular culture we preserve this meaning when we speak of art critics or movie critics: Siskel and Ebert *criticize* movies, but they may give a movie a "thumbs up" as well as a "thumbs down."

Biblical criticism is simply the attempt to make judgments about the text of the Bible—where it came from, who wrote it, and how is it to be understood. The *Anchor Bible Dictionary*, an excellent source of information on current biblical scholarship, defines biblical criticism this way:

Biblical criticism ... is the practice of analyzing and making discriminating judgments about the literature of the Bible—its origin, transmission, and interpretation. In this context, "criticism" has no negative connotation but, as in other fields, is designed to promote discriminating analysis and understanding.

(O'Neill 1992, 1:725-26)

Biblical criticism sprouted in the seventeenth and eighteenth centuries, came to fruition in the nineteenth and early twentieth centuries, and has been harvested ever since. Ironically, biblical criticism is even responsible for the rise of Christian fundamentalism, which arose in the early twentieth century in reaction to the growing use of biblical criticism among Christians. Although we realize today that a very basic form of criticism was employed by the early church in its choosing which books to include in the New Testament, the disciplined examination of the Bible and its contents could not be undertaken until the methods of critical-historical study in general developed. And as we saw in chapter 1, the discipline of history did not fully develop in the academy until the nineteenth century.

Let me restate this very important point. Our ancestors in faith could not have read the Bible through the eyes of biblical criticism, any more than our national ancestors could have developed an atomic bomb to use against the British during the American Revolution. Developing a nuclear weapon presupposes a theoretical knowledge of physics and a technological proficiency that were not present before our century. Likewise, reading the Bible critically presupposes a certain knowledge and methodological sophistication that were not available in earlier centuries. We can, of course, simply ignore the developments that gave rise to biblical criticism. We can deceive ourselves into thinking that what scholars have learned about the Bible and the cultures in which the Bible arose is irrelevant to faith. But doing so would be as foolhardy as a nation's proceeding in its foreign policy today by pretending that nuclear weapons do not exist.

Applying the methods of critical history to the Bible presupposes that it is a document that is a product of human history. The Bible did not one day drop from heaven. We're learning more and more about the process by which the Bible came to be, including the origin of the individual books and the decisions leading to the canonical collection of books. But we're learning these things precisely because we're looking at the Bible as we would any document. In 1860 a groundbreaking book was published in England. Entitled *Essays and Reviews*, this collection of essays appeared just a year after Charles Darwin's *Origin of Species*. In *Essays and Reviews*, the eminent Greek scholar Benjamin Jowett proclaimed the principle that I advocate, with these simple words: *"Interpret the Scripture like any other book"* (Jowett 1860, 377). In Jowett's day this was a radical proposal, so radical that the impact of Darwin's book on the intellectual world was delayed by the brouhaha over *Essays and Reviews*. But today this basic principle of biblical criticism is the foundation for most biblical scholarship outside the camp of biblical inerrantists. However, if we Christians today understand the Bible to be the Word of God, we must do so while recognizing it to be a product of human history. It's a wonderfully diverse record of Israel's and the earliest church's understandings of human life in the context of God. Through its pages, one can see developing, the notions of God that come to be central: first, in Israel's faith, then, in Jesus' teachings, and, finally, in earliest Christianity. In its pages one can see how the early church interpreted Jesus in light of Jewish messianic expectations and the sacrificial system that was part and parcel of first-century religion in Judea. We confront in scripture the foundational ways of thinking that generated the religious traditions of Judaism and Christianity. We encounter in scripture our forebears' witness to the reality of God as experienced in their day and time, expressed as best they could. But we do not encounter in scripture the particular words of God. The Word of God, the reality of God in our day and time, can only be encountered in scripture after we have taken seriously its historicity by recognizing that scripture arose in particular historical settings and that the way God is described therein is largely a result of the particular ideas, images, and ways of thinking of our ancestors in faith.

The recognition that God's Word can only be discerned in the midst of the human words of scripture liberates us from a constraining biblicism. To illustrate this point, let's look at Deuteronomy 20. First, let me set the context.

Deuteronomy was traditionally understood to be the fifth and final of the so-called Books of Moses, called by Christians the Pentateuch and by Jews, the Torah. Our ancestors took for granted that Moses was their author, but critical biblical scholars today recognize these books to be collections of diverse material written over about a four-hundred-year period of Israel's history. The book of Deuteronomy is constructed around three supposed speeches of Moses to the people of Israel encamped in the Transjordan prior to their entry into the Promised Land. In these speeches, Moses repeats some of the legal material that was earlier depicted as having been given to Moses by God on Mount Sinai. But again, critical scholars believe Deuteronomy to have been written much after Moses' time. In it one can see the continuing attempt of later Israelites to reinterpret the Mosaic traditions for their day. The Deuteronomic Reform of King Josiah in 621 B.C.E., which most scholars see as the impetus for this reinterpretation, is an interesting story in itself, but the details of that reform are not necessary for purposes of this illustration.

In Deuteronomy, Moses lays before the people "statutes and ordinances" that the Lord gave to him. In chapter 20, the statutes and ordinances are about waging war against Israel's enemies. The operative distinction in the passage we will examine is between the rules for waging war against enemy cities that are "very far from you" and those cities which are the "towns of these peoples that the LORD your God is giving you as an inheritance," that is, the cities in the promised land that are possessed by the Canaanites and other groups:

> When you draw near to a town to fight against it, offer it terms of peace. If it accepts your terms of peace and surrenders to you, then all the people in it shall serve you at forced labor. If it does not submit to you peacefully, but makes war against you, then you shall besiege it; and when the LORD your God gives it into your hand, you shall put all its males to the sword. You may, how-

ever, take as your booty the women, the children, livestock, and everything else in the town, all its spoil. You may enjoy the spoil of your enemies, which the LORD your God has given you. Thus you shall treat all the towns that are very far from you, which are not towns of the nations here. But as for the towns of these peoples that the LORD your God is giving you as an inheritance, you must not let anything that breathes remain alive. You shall annihilate them—the Hittites and the Amorites, the Canaanites and the Perizzites, the Hivites and the Jebusites—just as the LORD your God has commanded, so that they may not teach you to do all the abhorrent things that they do for their gods, and you thus sin against the LORD your God. (Deuteronomy 20:10-18)

In this passage Moses supposedly conveys the divine conventions for warfare: in cities outside the promised land, only the males are executed when the city is defeated; women and children are prizes of war and can be taken off in slavery. But in the promised land itself, a conquered city is to be utterly annihilated. All people—men, women, and children—and all animals are to be executed. Why? So none will lead the Israelites to stray from strict worship of the Lord God. Today, we call this way of fighting a war *ethnic cleansing*. In recent times we have seen such an approach to war in Bosnia, where annihilation of enemies was seen by the combatants as their duty and calling. But civilized nations stood appalled at the massacres that went on in that civil war. And yet our own Bible says God advocated such an ethnic cleansing of the Canaanites.

How are we to deal with this passage and the many others like it in our Bible? One response, that of certain fundamentalists today, is to say: the Bible says it, and I believe it. Since the Bible is inerrant, God really commanded the slaughter of all those people. Who are we to judge what God commands? Who are we to question the wisdom or morality of the Almighty Deity?

But God is worthy of worship not just because God is powerful, but because God is good. What do we do to our faith when we willingly attribute to God moral characteristics that we find abhorrent in our fellow humans? Moreover, there's the problem of consistency. The God of whom Jesus spoke had very different characteristics from those of this God portrayed in Deuteronomy. How can we hold that Deuteronomy's portrait of God is consistent with Jesus' portrait of God?

A way many of our ancestors answered this question was to appeal to the notion of *dispensations*. God had one covenant with the Israelites and the terms of that covenant were very different from the terms of the covenant he came to have with the church. After all, Deuteronomy is part of the Old Testament, the *old* covenant; we live today under a new covenant by which God has chosen to relate to humankind. Under that old covenant, God did want his people the Israelites totally to annihilate those whose land he had promised to them. But under the new, God chooses to relate to us differently. Now we are to "love your enemies and pray for those who persecute you" (Matthew 5:44). Although this appeal to different covenants is a happier solution to our problem than simply the "Bible-says-it-I-believe-it" approach, it still raises a fundamental theological question: Was God not, from the very beginning of creation, a God whose love encompasses all of God's creatures? Could God's fundamental relation to creation so dramatically change over time?

A more satisfactory answer can be found using the tools of biblical criticism. What we have in Deuteronomy is not a direct report of God's commandments to the Israelites but a report of what ancient Israelites believed about God in their historical context. The words are human words, words of an ancient people who understood deity in light of the values and moralities of an ancient world. Utter annihilation of enemies was an accepted code of war. The notion of innocent women and children wasn't part of their way of thinking, for the notion of innocent noncombatants developed later in Western civilization. However, thinking of God in this way was consistent with the way that great human leaders were envisioned. A great leader of a tribal people in the ancient Near East had to be a warrior leader who preserved his own people at all costs against their enemies.

Should it surprise us that, using the ways of thinking and ideas of their time, some ancient Israelites thought of God in the limited terms of their ancient worldview?

Humans can talk about God only by using the historical ways of thought available to them; this is well illustrated in other periods of biblical history. For example, during the time when Israel settled down into cities and developed a political system dependent on kingship, the Israelites conceived God in terms of a king. During the heyday of Judah and the dominance of Jerusalem in Near Eastern affairs, God was conceived as inhabitant and protector of Jerusalem. Other examples could be adduced as further proof that what we have in the Bible is a record of our ancestors' understandings of God, understandings that have to be taken seriously by us since they constitute part of our inheritance. But taking them seriously means understanding them in the historical context in which they arose, not taking them literally as the direct, unmediated revelation of God's specific words. Only in this way will we discern God's Word within the Bible's words.

THE CREATION NARRATIVES IN GENESIS

A look at the creation stories in Genesis will be helpful for tying together the strands of my argument up to this point. To take completely seriously what we've learned in science about the origins of the universe and life on Earth, what we've learned historically about the ancient cultures in which the biblical stories of creation arose, and what we know today about the character of the Bible and how it came to be, gives us a perspective on these first chapters of Genesis that our ancestors in faith could not have had.

First, biblical criticism has taught us that there are two different stories of creation in the first two chapters of Genesis. The first story, in Genesis 1:1–2:4a, depicts creation as an ordered six-day process. God creates by speaking: "God said 'Let there be X' ... and it was so"—just fill in the X with the various things created: light, a dome to separate waters, dry land, vegetation, lights in the dome, fish and birds, and land animals. At the end of this six-day process, God creates humankind, "male and female he created them" (1:27). Then God rested on the seventh day. The second of the creation stories begins in Genesis 2:4*b* and runs through the end of chapter 3. In this story, God "formed man from dust of the ground, and breathed into his nostrils the breath of life" (2:7). God then plants a garden for the man, creates animals for the man in an attempt to find a suitable companion, but failing that, causes a deep sleep to fall upon the man and takes a rib from his side from which to form a woman. The man—in Hebrew *'adam*, from which we get the English proper name Adam—and his wife Eve are tempted by the serpent, disobey God's command not to eat of the tree in the middle of the garden, and end up being tossed out of the garden God planted for them.

Even a layperson reading these stories today can see striking differences in the accounts: in Genesis 1, humankind is created both male and female at the end of the six days; in Genesis 2, the man is created at the outset of the story before plants and animals and the woman is created at the end. Moreover, the very language of the two stories is different: Genesis 1 uses lofty and liturgical language while Genesis 2 is much more storylike and simple. The initial states of things at the outset of the stories are dramatically different: in Genesis 1, it is the waters of chaos; in Genesis 2 it is dry, arid land. And the deity is called different names in these two stories—in Genesis 1 the deity is simply called God (Hebrew, *elohim*) while in Genesis 2, the deity is consistently referred to by the name given to him by the Israelites: Yahweh.[1]

Our ancestors in faith began with the assumption that the Pentateuch was the work of Moses. Hence, even though the narratives in chapters 1 and 2 told different stories, they read them

---

1. In most English versions, translators, following a long practice in Judaism that replaces the divine name with the honorific title *Lord* when reading the text, use LORD to render the name *Yahweh*. However, they indicate this substitution by printing LORD in small capitals, making it possible for the reader to know when the divine name appears in the Hebrew.

as complementary. For example, Martin Luther, the initiator of the Protestant Reformation in the sixteenth century, reads the story in Genesis 2 as explication of the six days of creation in chapter 1, so that the planting of the garden in 2:8-9 is seen as "belonging to the work of the third day" and the forming of man from dust of the ground, as "refer[ring] to the work of the sixth day" (Luther 1958, 43). It never enters Luther's mind that Moses might not be the author of the Pentateuch and that Genesis 1 and 2 might be different stories, because such notions were not options in Luther's thought world.

A few voices, as early as the eleventh century, had raised questions about the Mosaic authorship of all parts of the Pentateuch, but the question did not begin to receive serious attention until the seventeenth century (Friedman 1987, 18-21). Thomas Hobbes in his *Leviathan* of 1651 challenged the Mosaic authorship of the entirety of the Pentateuch, even though he accepted that Moses did indeed write many portions of it (1962, chap. 33). Soon after, in 1670, Baruch Spinoza anonymously published his *Theologico-Political Treatise* in which he concludes that "it is thus clearer than the sun at noonday that the Pentateuch was not written by Moses but by someone who lived long after Moses" (Spinoza 1951, 1:124).

Over the next two centuries, scholars moved from the simple recognition that the Pentateuch was not all from Moses' hand to the actual identification of the various sources that were combined to form the Pentateuch. By the late–nineteenth century, biblical scholars proposed that four main sources, stemming from different hands at different times of Israel's history, were combined to form the Pentateuch as we know it. Moreover, they showed that little of this material was attributable to Moses himself. This theory that four sources were combined to form the Pentateuch is known as the Documentary Hypothesis. Though scholars still argue about details of this theory, mainline biblical scholarship accepts what historians can teach us about the evolution of the text of the Pentateuch.

How does the Documentary Hypothesis help us read the first two chapters of Genesis? It suggests that the two stories of creation are from two different sources in Israel's history. Scholars believe Genesis 1:1–2:4a to have been written during the period of the Exile in the sixth century B.C.E. It is believed to come from what scholars call the "P" source, which is so named due to the interest this material shows in priestly matters. As such, it is among the latest material collected into the Pentateuch and reflects aspects of the Babylonian stories of creation with which the exiled Jews in Babylon would have been very familiar. In contrast, the story of Adam and Eve in chapter 2 is from the earliest of the four sources, called the "J" source, named because this source uses the divine name *Yahweh* (in German, *Jahwe* hence the "J") from the very beginning to describe God. The source called "J" is believed to have arisen during the period in which David and Solomon ruled Israel in the tenth century B.C.E. It is a simpler narrative, more storylike in character, and it depicts Yahweh as an active participant in the plot: he walks in the garden, he brings animals to Adam, he takes a rib from Adam's side, he confronts Adam and Eve with their nakedness, and he debates with Adam and Eve over their actions. Recent biblical scholarship teaches us that these two creation narratives certainly weren't written by Moses but rather stem from different times and different groups in Israel's history. That's why they are different. They are different stories about how things came to be—stories told in primitive cultures that did not have our modern scientific understanding of the universe, its structure, and its origin. This is what we've learned of the creation stories in Genesis as a result of modern historical and literary research.

Once we've given up the attempt to make scientific sense out of the stories, we can then ask how these stories still create for us as Christians a way of seeing the world that we also know through science. And here two central affirmations about the way we see the world through the eyes of faith are crucial. First, these stories, especially the first story in Genesis 1, portray God as the sole source of all that is. Unlike the Babylonian stories of creation from which the authors of Genesis 1 draw, monotheism pervades the narratives in Genesis. In the Babylonian stories there are many gods involved in the creation of things; but in Israel's story there is but one God who brings all into being. The first affirmation that comes from the biblical accounts of creation is this: the world and everything in it are from God. And God stands within and behind the world as its very source and very structure.

A second faith affirmation grows out of the first story: God created all that is as *good*. Here again, our Israelite forebears had insight into a way of seeing the world that was rejected by many other religions of their day. Evil is most easily explained as originating in a divine being in opposition to God. Many ancient cosmogonies, or myths of creation, took precisely this way of dealing with evil: part of the creation was of the evil god; hence evil is a part of created nature. But Israel affirmed that God is the only God there is. There is no opposing deity; the world as it is created by the one God is good: "God saw everything that he had made, and indeed, it was very good ..." (Genesis 1:31). In faith we view the world and our lives within the world as undergirded by the goodness of God, what we call God's grace. We may understand the process whereby the universe evolved rather differently from our forebears, but we share with them the conviction that God and God's grace underlie our lives in this world. However we struggle with evil, we must finally as Christians see it as subordinate to and powerless in the face of God's all-encompassing grace.

Those two fundamental affirmations grow out of our tradition's myths of creation. Biblical criticism has helped us see the true character of these stories and their relation to the myths of the ancient world. Science has given us a good picture of the actual physical process that has led to the present state of our universe. But faith enables us to see this universe and the history that lies behind it as being of God's grace. For Christians, however, such a faith in God's grace rests on more than simply our faith in creation. It is fundamentally constituted by our appropriation of Jesus' way of seeing God, to which I'll turn in the next chapter.

CHAPTER FIVE

THINKING OVER THE SIGNIFICANCE OF JESUS

*C*hristians' faith is rooted in images of Jesus Christ; it always has been and it always will be. In and through the biblical images of Jesus, we learn to image God. But standing where we do at the watershed of the modern and postmodern worlds, we cannot see Jesus as did our forebears in faith. Every generation, of course, has had to come to grips with who Jesus is. But recent generations do so in the context I've set out in the foregoing chapters. Here especially the modern tools of historical research and our recognition of the nature of the Bible force many of us to rethink the orthodox claims about Jesus' character and metaphysical status. As we today think of Jesus Christ, we do so in a context very different from those of Christians in past centuries.

Earlier Christians were able to accept the story of Jesus as presented in the Bible as an accurate depiction of what he said, what he did, and who he was. The gospel authors were assumed to report accurately from either their own firsthand experiences of Jesus or from eyewitnesses' reports to them. By the time orthodox christological claims were solidified in the fourth and fifth centuries, Christians typically saw Trinitarianism and Chalcedonian Christology—the doctrines that Jesus is the second person of the eternal Trinity and that he is to be understood as fully human *and* fully divine—in the gospel texts as they read them.

Only with the development of critical history was it possible to begin to ask modern questions of the gospels and to distinguish clearly between Jesus as he was recoverable by historical research and the images of Jesus that developed in the early church. During the nineteenth century there was great hope that the new tools of critical history would provide the key to unlocking the *real* Jesus from the confines of later Christian traditions about him. But those nineteenth-century quests for the historical Jesus did not succeed. As Albert Schweitzer pointed out in his famous study of the quest for the historical Jesus, the many different portraits of the "historical" Jesus that emerged from different historians, ended up looking very much like the ideas of Jesus that the historians had before they started out on their quests (Schweitzer 1968).

Though we've been unable fully to uncover the historical Jesus, we have learned a great deal over the past two centuries about our New Testament, how it came to be written, who wrote it, and when it came into its present form. As Christians, we must take this new knowledge seriously, even when it complicates the assumptions our forebears in the faith were able to make. Let me simply review the main conclusions that are well accepted among scholars trained in the critical study of the Bible. We must again keep in mind that fundamentalist biblical scholars reject biblical criticism; for them, the Bible is inerrant. Everything in it—at least in the original manuscripts—was basically dictated by God; hence it cannot be treated like a document that arose in human history. But most biblical scholars today do not begin with inerrantist presuppositions, and such scholars cover the entire Christian spectrum—from Roman Catholics, to Presbyterians, to Episcopalians, to Disciples of Christ, to United Methodists, and to Baptists. They would virtually all concur in the following well-established conclusion of modern biblical research: *The gospels are not eyewitness accounts of Jesus' life and teachings but are second-generation narratives that are proclamations of the earliest churches' post-Easter faith.* The gospels were written in early church communities during the last third of the first century. None was written by an eyewitness to Jesus' life. Only two of the gospels are even traditionally attributed to Jesus' twelve disciples, namely, the Gospels of Matthew and John. The gospel we call Mark was attributed to a companion of Peter by an early church historian. Luke is traditionally attributed to a companion of Paul. Luke, however, is the only gospel that tells us something of its origin. We often overlook the very interesting opening verses of Luke's Gospel:

> Since many have undertaken to set down an orderly account of the events that have been fulfilled among us, just as they were handed on to us by those who from the beginning were eyewitnesses and servants of the word, I too decided, after investigating everything carefully from the very first, to write an orderly account for you, most excellent Theophilus, so that you may know the truth concerning the things about which you have been instructed. (Luke 1:1-4)

Note that this gospel itself tells us that it is not by an eyewitness but by one who received the stories from those who were eyewitnesses. Also notice that the author admits the existence of other narratives of the events "that have been fulfilled among us." He is concerned to present an "orderly account," implying that he wasn't satisfied with those accounts already in existence. Although the author names the patron to whom he addresses his introduction, he does not name himself anywhere in the gospel or in the book of Acts, for which he is also responsible. And this is true of the other three gospels: none are internally identified as being written by those persons whose names appear in their titles. It appears that the association with particular apostles only comes about in the second century. Historically, therefore, we must conclude that the four gospels are anonymous and that it is early church tradition rather than the character of the gospels themselves, or a claim to authorship found within those gospels, that led to the titles by which Christians have known them for centuries.

Not only are the gospels written decades after Jesus' life, they are the early church's preaching about Jesus' significance to believers and not what we would consider biographies in the modern sense of the word. Their intention is to proclaim the good news about Jesus and persuade their readers to follow in the Way, which was an early designation for the Jesus movement. Our four canonical gospels, along with other early gospels that were not collected in our canonical New Testament, such as the Gospel of Thomas, are virtually our sole sources for reconstructing a portrait of Jesus of Nazareth. Regrettably, no contemporaneous non-Christian documents about him exist. The earliest references to Jesus in non-Christian sources speak only indirectly of Jesus, identifying him as the founder of the groups of which the authors are directly aware. But these references all arise decades after Jesus' life, the earliest at about the same time as the gospels themselves.[1]

Because they are the early church's proclamation about Jesus, the gospels cannot be read as accurate transcriptions of what Jesus said or historical accounts of what he did. And this is the most significant difference between our reading of the gospels and that of our ancestors in the faith. Our ancestors could take the gospel narratives simply as presentations of what Jesus did and said. They were aware, of course, that the four gospels differ and that different versions of events are contained within the gospel narratives. But because they approached the gospels with assumptions different from those of modern critical biblical scholarship, they did not see the differences as we see them, and instead saw great harmonies within the gospels, such that all the different narratives of Jesus' life and teachings could be fitted into a seamless whole. As I argued in chapter 1, we can only think in *our* time and *our* place, utilizing the tools that are available to us. So also our ancestors could only do, and they are not to be criticized for the historical limitations of their thought. But we now know that the gospels are not eyewitness accounts of Jesus' life but second-

---

1. For an excellent brief summary of the evidence from non-Christian sources, see Kee 1990, 6-19. For a more exhaustive analysis, see Meier 1991– , 1:56-111.

generation narratives written by believers whose thoughts were based on traditions that had been handed down to them from eyewitnesses and other believers. We also know that even the eyewitnesses to Jesus' life saw him differently after Easter. Mark's Gospel portrays the disciples as failing to see who Jesus really was. Indeed, they all abandon him after he is arrested. Mark's view of the gospel is summed up in the words of the Roman centurion who recognizes, after witnessing Jesus' death on the cross, that "truly this man was God's Son" (Mark 15:39). Only on the completion of the whole story did Jesus' significance become clear. Easter thus transformed the followers of Jesus so that they looked back on all they had experienced in a new way. We are told the story of Jesus from the perspective of the new faith that arose after Easter. It is a story literally infected with the new understanding of Jesus' significance and the enthusiasm of the new believers who were willing to give up all they had to follow in his Way.

For us today the hope is gone that the gospels convey simply and directly the actual words and deeds of Jesus, though there is no question that this man's life and teaching were the foundation on top of which the gospel traditions developed.[2] We might think of each gospel as an iced layer cake. The actual words and deeds of Jesus are foundational ingredients in the gospel batter,

---

2. The Jesus Seminar, a group of New Testament scholars meeting under the aegis of the Westar Institute, has produced a translation of the gospels (including the noncanonical Gospel of Thomas) and has color-coded all the sayings attributed to Jesus. The color-coding represents statistically the members' judgments of the likelihood that the historical Jesus really said what the gospels attributed him to have said. Those sayings that are highly likely to have been actually spoken by Jesus are coded in red; those that were most likely to stem from later church traditions are coded in black; and the colors pink and gray are used to code passages that fall between the red and black extremes. Looking at a copy of *The Five Gospels*, one is struck by the rarity of red passages and the abundance of gray and black passages. But this shouldn't be surprising, given that we now understand the gospels to be early church proclamation, shaped by the church's growing diversity of ways of expressing Jesus' significance to those who followed in the Way. (See Funk, Hoover, and The Jesus Seminar 1993.)

but so too are eyewitnesses' interpretations of Jesus and what he said. These memories and traditions were cooked in early church communities for decades before the authors of our gospels each used them in composing his gospel within his particular community's perspective and out of his own particular interpretation of Jesus. Since there are four different gospels, we can get a grasp on the particular perspective of each gospel author by comparing the gospel accounts with one another. So each author's view of his gospel is like the icing on the cake: as an ingredient it is easily scraped off and separated from the finished pastry. But the actual words and deeds of Jesus, and the originating interpretations of the original eyewitnesses, are more like the flour and baking soda: one can't easily separate them after they've been baked in a cake.

THE EXISTENTIAL SIGNIFICANCE OF JESUS

Having recognized the character of the gospels as early Christian proclamation and not objective history, we are left with a burning question: How then can we think of Jesus if the gospels themselves are not historically accurate accounts of his life and teachings? Many, I'm sure, will think that the appropriate conclusion to be drawn from modern scholarship is that Christianity is groundless and ought be given up as a viable way of faith today. Others, because of the paralyzing effects of the historical uncertainties surrounding the critical study of the gospels, will opt for a fundamentalistic acceptance of the literal truth of the Bible. This latter approach withdraws the New Testament from the scrutiny of modern critical thought and preserves its seeming purity only by refusing to take seriously the differing narratives of Jesus' life. But I seek a middle way that recognizes the validity of research into the historical questions that surround the life of this historical figure and the movement that arose following his death, and yet also recognizes that the answers to these questions really don't get to the heart of Christians' faith.

Such a middle way must begin with the recognition that religious faith is not about historical events in the past or eschatological events in the future but is about our lives here and now and the way that we see our lives in the ultimate context of God. What is religiously significant is not who Jesus *was,* but who Jesus *is* as a living spirit in the hearts of those who follow in his way of love. One of the great developments in Christian theology this century was the willingness to state forthrightly that Christian faith is about our existence before God in the present and not simply about some hoped-for life in the hereafter. Utilizing the philosophical thought of Martin Heidegger, theologians like Rudolf Bultmann and Paul Tillich set out to reinterpret much of the classical Christian tradition in existentialistic terms, seeing Jesus' significance as the one who confronts us with the possibility of living authentically (Bultmann 1958) or as presenting the possibility of New Being that overcomes the estrangement between humankind and God (Tillich 1967). For these theologians, and many others like them, Christian faith is about a way of being in the world.

The significance of Jesus in Christians' faith is not historical but existential; or, as Schubert Ogden so aptly puts it, the subject of our religious assertions about Jesus "is not Jesus in his being in himself, but rather Jesus in his meaning for us" (1982, 62). *In his meaning for us.* Whatever can or cannot be said about Jesus as a historical figure, Christians' faith today is fundamentally shaped by the encounter with Jesus as a living spirit, a living image, within the churches' proclamations of God's grace. Earlier in this century, theologians expressed this existential meaning of Jesus by distinguishing between the Jesus of history and the Christ of faith. The true object of our worship as Christians, they said, is not some elusive historical reconstruction of Jesus but the Christ proclaimed as the one encountered by believers in the preaching of the church, in the narratives of scripture, and in the spiritual life. I find this distinction inadequate and too simplistic: *Christ* is a title given to Jesus by earlier followers and it is only one such title that was used to express the existential significance of Jesus to the early Christians. Nonetheless, what underlies this distinction is what I'm trying to explicate by referring to Jesus' existential significance for believers as different from his significance as a historical figure in the past.

Existential significance is a relational quality dependent on our human imaginative capabilities. As I write these lines, my wife is miles away visiting her family. Yet it makes perfectly good sense to say that I presently love my wife, that she means the world to me, even though she is not physically present. I am able to do so because she is present to me in memory and imagination. Even when she is physically present, it is not just her physical presence to which I fundamentally relate; her physical presence is but an underlying component of her existential presence. And the memories of her, all we have done with each other, and all that we have been through together over the past twenty-five years are intimately bound up with who she is for me even as she stands before me in physical presence.

My wife teaches preschool. She has become a very important person for those three-year-olds in her class. But her significance to them is different from her significance to me. The way they would describe her would involve their relationship to her, just as the way I would describe her would involve her relationship to me. At the level of physical description, we might describe her in the same way—if we compensate for the imaginative creativity of preschoolers! But as for those dimensions of her that only exist in relationship to us, that is, when we get to those aspects of her that have to do with her existential significance to us, then our descriptions will differ significantly. Her roles as preschool teacher and as spouse shape the differing ways we would describe her.

Christian claims about Jesus are existential claims, not historical claims. When Christians called Jesus the Christ, when they came to proclaim him as son of God, and when they talked of his miracles and exorcisms, they were expressing his existential significance, utilizing the images and terms available for such description in their cultural milieu. Those eyewitnesses to Jesus' life who became the proclaimers of Jesus' significance expressed that significance with images and symbols of first-century Judaism. As the message about Jesus spread into different regions with different communities of believers, especially after the eye-witnesses themselves were dead, the images of Jesus conveyed through the preaching of the church, the telling of stories about Jesus, and the passing on of his teachings began to vary. Different believers came to understand Jesus' significance in different ways; when they told the stories and proclaimed his significance in preaching, the stories came to be shaped and the preaching molded to best express the particular significance that Jesus had to the different communities.

NEW TESTAMENT PORTRAITS OF JESUS

The New Testament itself witnesses to this process of diverging interpretations of Jesus' significance. Paul's Letter to the Galatians, written in the mid-50s, angrily denounces the Christians in this region for "turning to a different gospel" (Galatians 1:6). Paul has preached his understanding of Jesus to the churches in Galatia. A significant part of Paul's understanding involves the claim that all people can follow Jesus, regardless of whether or not they are Jews first. However, Paul learns that others have visited the church in Galatia preaching that one must become a Jew first to follow Jesus and that Jesus' significance is limited to those who are Jews. He rejects this "other gospel" and chastises the Galatians for listening to an interpretation of Jesus other than his.

The very collection of books that compose the New Testament is further witness to the diversity of meanings that Jesus came to have among the early followers. It is significant that the New Testament contains *four* gospels, especially when these gospels are read closely to reveal their different interpretations of Jesus' significance. These four gospels, as critical-historical study has now taught us, come from different communities within the early church. These different communities saw Jesus' significance in different ways. Since most scholars believe that the authors of Matthew and Luke used a copy of Mark as a source for their gospels, the differences among the synoptic interpretations of Jesus' significance are small when compared with John's interpretation. Whereas the Synoptics depict Jesus' significance primarily in terms of his preaching about God's kingdom, John's Gospel expresses Jesus' significance by portraying him as one who proclaims himself as the only mediator to the Father (John 14:6) and as the eternal Word of God become flesh (John 1:1). In John, Jesus is depicted as the very presence of God's reality. There is no future, coming kingdom of God in John's view of Jesus. Likewise, John's Gospel contains no story of the ascension of Jesus to heaven, which in Luke's story of Jesus sets up the need for Jesus to return again when God's kingdom is brought about. Instead, John's Gospel implies the continuing presence of Jesus living among believers. A careful reading of the gospels will reveal this and many other differences in the way that the authors portray Jesus' significance.

But the differences in the portraits of Jesus in the gospels and Paul pale in comparison with the differences between the Jesus of the gospels and the portrait of the returning Jesus painted by the author of the Revelation to John. When, in Matthew, one of Jesus' disciples strikes out with a sword at the high priest's servant who was among those who had come to arrest Jesus in Gethsemane, Jesus angrily denounces the sword-bearer: "Put your sword back into its place; for all who take the sword will perish by the sword" (Matthew 26:52). This passage is consistent with the gospels' witness to Jesus' pacifism and attitude toward his enemies. But the author of the Revelation to John, writing in a very different situation, interprets Jesus' significance in a radically contrasting way. In this book Jesus is himself depicted as the sword-bearer, who, when he returns to earth in his second coming, will slay the enemies of the church with his own sword: "From his mouth comes a sharp sword with which to strike down the nations, and he will rule them with a rod of iron; he will tread the wine press of the fury of the wrath of God the Almighty." Indeed, the nations of unbelievers will be "killed by the sword of the rider on the horse, the sword that came from his mouth; and all the birds were gorged with their flesh" (Revelation 19:15, 21). God's fury, God's wrath, the returned Jesus as massacrer of unbelievers—these images in the book of Revelation are in fundamental tension with the images of Jesus found in the gospels.

But isn't this just what one might expect from the New Testament, since it was compiled from different writings produced by early Christians? Historically we now know that the books that came together to form our New Testament originated in different communities in early Christianity. A chief criterion by which they were included in the canon was their supposed apostolicity, which means that they stemmed from those who were eyewitnesses to Jesus. But modern biblical scholarship has concluded that *none* of the writings in our New Testament is apostolic in this sense. Even Paul, the author of the earliest writings in the New Testament, never claims to have seen the historical Jesus, only the risen Jesus in his vision on the road to Damascus. All of the New Testament writings are witnesses of faith by those who were second- and third-generation believers. And by the second and third generations, expressions of the significance of Jesus to believers had already begun to diverge. What the New Testament collects together is a diversity of witnesses to the significance of Jesus. There is no single biblical portrait of Jesus, only portraits of him in light of different interpretations of his significance. Here again, if we are to be thinking Christians who take completely seriously what modern history teaches, then we simply cannot make the assumptions about the apostolicity of the New Testament that our forebears could make. What then are we to do?

What we have to do is much the same thing our forebears did, often unconsciously: we find within the biblical witnesses to Jesus' significance certain key images grounded in key biblical passages, and these then become normative for the way we appropriate and read the rest of scripture. Unlike our forebears, however, we must proceed knowing that there is no single truth to scripture, but its truth is multivalent and depends on the believer's particular stance as he or she approaches scripture. We must find that image or set of images that becomes normative for us, while yet allowing other Christians to do the same. In this sense, the many denominations with their different approaches to Christian faith are but different interpretative communities in which particular images and ways of seeing Jesus' significance come to the fore.

Here we must be careful to avoid the trap of a false objectivism. The "us" is an essential component of the expression "Jesus' significance for us." It is not that Jesus' significance is something objective apart from any human appropriation of it; nor is it a matter of various believers *expressing* in different ways some single metaphysical significance to Jesus. The different expressions of the significance of Jesus to us will vary with the particular group expressing such significance. Hence the very meanings of Jesus are plural. Here again, the postmodern situation in which we stand, with its emphasis on the plurality of meanings, will fundamentally shape our appropriations of Jesus' significance, and there is no way around the essential plurality of meanings with which we now have to deal.

Our task today is to hammer out and shape our own images of Jesus, images that grow out of and are in dialogue with the images of our forebears in faith, but ones that speak to us in our current situation. We do this, of course, in dialogue with believers in the past and others in the present who see Jesus differently. But certainly the originating witnesses to Jesus' significance who are found in the New Testament are primary dialogue partners. For it was from the significance that Jesus had to the originating witnesses that all later interpretations arose. Before I lay out my own understanding of the significance of Jesus for us today, let's look at some of the images and symbols that the earliest witnesses used to describe Jesus' significance.

As we think about the earliest symbols used to express Jesus' significance to believers, we must remember that Jesus and his early followers were Jews, a fact that has come today to be especially appreciated as a result of historical attempts to situate Jesus in his cultural context. To read the gospels with awareness of the Jewish roots of its message is to gain new appreciation for the symbols that his early followers used to express his significance.

Certainly one of the earliest symbols to be applied to Jesus by his followers was *Messiah*. *Messiah* comes from the Hebrew word *mashiah*, which literally means "anointed one." Anointing, the symbolic act of pouring of oil over the head, was the way that Saul, David, Solomon, and the other kings of Israel and Judah were made king.

The background significance of this Hebrew idea is partly lost to us, because both the Hebrew word *mashiah* and the equivalent Greek word *christos* are not translated but transliterated into the English words *Messiah* and *Christ*. Both *mashiah* and *christos* mean *the anointed one* in Hebrew and Greek, respectively. But *Christ* comes to be so routinely associated with Jesus that we forget that it is a title and not Jesus' last name. Many Jews in first-century Palestine hoped for a new leader to arise in the Davidic lineage who would reestablish the throne of David and take back control of Judea from the Romans, who had occupied her since 63 B.C.E. These hopes for one chosen of God to come to the people and bring them back to the prestige and power they enjoyed in the great days of David and Solomon were alive in Jesus' day. Jesus' followers used this Jewish image to proclaim his significance.[3]

But this involved a fundamental reconstruction of that inherited notion of messiah, for Jesus was not a political figure who desired control of Judea. And his rejection by the Judean leaders

---

3. See Collins 1995 for an excellent discussion of the different messianic images present in first-century Judaism.

of his day and finally his execution by the despicable method of Roman crucifixion surely confirmed his failure to be a messiah in the traditional view. But after Easter his followers came to reinterpret the expectations of a messiah through the images of the Suffering Servant of the Lord found in the portions of the book of Isaiah which stem from the anonymous exilic prophet scholars call Second Isaiah. So the preaching that the early followers of Jesus did as the movement spread throughout Judea, then into Samaria, and then across the Eastern Mediterranean, proclaimed this new understanding of messiah as a sort of spiritual, rather than political king. But this symbol was rooted in the experience of those first-century Jews who were Jesus' earliest followers.

Another pattern of thought from first-century Judaism was used by Jesus' earliest followers to describe his significance: Jesus was seen as an atoning sacrifice for sin. The religion of ancient Israel was a sacrificial religion and sacrifices continued in first-century Judaism. Because we tend to read the Old Testament from our Christian perspective, we often fail to realize what a central role animal and grain sacrifices played in Jewish rituals. Covenants in ancient Israel were ratified by blood sacrifice: think of the ceremony in Exodus 24, in which Moses sacrifices oxen and then throws their blood on the gathered people saying, "See the blood of the covenant that the LORD has made with you in accordance with all these words" (Exodus 24:8); or the elaborate sacrifice of 22,000 oxen and 120,000 sheep that Solomon offered to the Lord when the Temple was dedicated (1 Kings 8:62-64). Why were these sacrifices important? Because the ancient Israelites believed that God wanted the sacrifices and that the people had to make these sacrifices to stay in good standing with their God. In the New Testament, the book of Hebrews, which interprets Jesus directly in light of the sacrificial practices of Judaism, sums up this ancient understanding when it says, "Under the law almost everything is purified with blood, and without the shedding of blood there is no forgiveness of sins" (Hebrews 9:22).

The most important sacrificial ritual for ancient Israel was celebrated on the Day of Atonement. On that day, the high priest in Israel would sacrifice a number of animals. Two goats would be chosen and lots would be drawn to determine the fate of each goat. One goat would be sacrificed and the blood from that goat would be sprinkled about the innermost sanctuary of the Temple for its cleansing effect. Leviticus 16:15-19 describes the ritual in this way:

> He shall slaughter the goat of the sin offering that is for the people and bring its blood inside the curtain, and do with its blood as he did with the blood of the bull, sprinkling it upon the mercy seat and before the mercy seat. Thus he shall make atonement for the sanctuary, because of the uncleannesses of the people of Israel, and because of their transgressions, all their sins; and so he shall do for the tent of meeting, which remains with them in the midst of their uncleannesses. No one shall be in the tent of meeting from the time he enters to make atonement in the sanctuary until he comes out and has made atonement for himself and for his house and for all the assembly of Israel. Then he shall go out to the altar that is before the LORD and make atonement on its behalf, and shall take some of the blood of the bull and of the blood of the goat, and put it on each of the horns of the altar. He shall sprinkle some of the blood on it with his finger seven times, and cleanse it and hallow it from the uncleannesses of the people of Israel.

The other goat, the scapegoat, receives from the priest's hands all the sins of the people, and that goat is cast out into the wilderness, thus symbolically taking the sins of the people with it.

Paul's authentic letters in the New Testament—Romans, 1 and 2 Corinthians, Galatians, Philippians, 1 Thessalonians, and Philemon—interpret Jesus' significance through the concepts of the Jewish sacrificial system. Paul is a Jew, and a Pharisee at that. He knows well the Jewish law, and that includes the Jewish ritual laws. For Paul, Jesus' significance lies in his death on the cross, a death which Paul sees in light of the sacrifice of atonement. Listen to the language by which Paul expresses Jesus' significance: "They are now justified by his grace as a gift, through the redemption that is in Christ Jesus, whom God put forward as a sacrifice of atonement by his blood, effective through faith" (Romans 3:24-25). Now certainly Paul understands that Jesus' sacrificial death is sufficient atonement for all persons. In this sense Jesus' death is, in the words of one traditional communion liturgy, "a full, perfect, and sufficient sacrifice for the sins of the whole world." We need not sacrifice for our sins because Jesus' sacrifice is sufficient. This blood atonement thinking becomes part and parcel of classical Christian orthodoxy and still holds a place in popular Christian expression. Just think how many gospel hymns wax lyrical about the cleansing power of Jesus' blood.

Though classical Christian doctrine recognized the sufficiency of Jesus' sacrifice and hence moved beyond the ancient Israelite sacrificial cult, did it really move beyond the ancient way of thinking about God as *requiring* such blood sacrifice? The notion of atonement, as that which brings about reconciliation between us and God, has been variously interpreted in Christian history. During the Middle Ages Anselm of Canterbury offered an explanation that came to dominate Western views of the atonement. In his view, human sin was an affront to God's honor. A satisfaction must take place to overcome the affront, but since human sin was an infinite affront in the face of God, God himself became a man, who, because he was perfect, could, in his sacrificial death, satisfy God's demand for justice (Anselm 1958).

BEYOND THE ATONEMENT TO GRACE

Both these ways of thinking of the atonement, as blood sacrifice and as satisfaction owed to God, see God as requiring something of us in order to be reconciled, something we aren't able to pay, so that it's paid on our behalf by Jesus. But what is the character of God that is implied by both these classical ways of talking about Jesus' significance in the images of blood atonement and satisfaction? Somehow, blood has to be spilled or satisfaction must be made to bring us into right relation to God. Hence these classical approaches to the atonement presuppose a God who demands blood or satisfaction before we can rightly relate to God. But an important image of God that Jesus presents in our gospels runs counter to these classical images. God's grace does not require anything to be paid for sin. It is a free gift, totally undeserved, totally unmerited.

Here, for me, the New Testament passages that become absolutely central are those in which Jesus describes God's grace. No better passage expresses this image of God than the parable of the prodigal son:

> Then Jesus said, "There was a man who had two sons. The younger of them said to his father, 'Father, give me the share of the property that will belong to me.' So he divided his property between them. A few days later the younger son gathered all he had and traveled to a distant country, and there he squandered his property in dissolute living. When he had spent everything, a severe famine took place throughout that country, and he began to be in need. So he went and hired himself out to one of the citizens of that country, who sent him to his fields to feed the pigs. He would gladly have filled himself with the pods that the pigs were eating; and no one gave him anything. But when he came to himself he said, 'How many of my father's hired hands have bread enough and to spare, but here I am dying of hunger! I will get up and go to my father, and I will say to him, "Father, I have sinned against heaven and before you; I am no longer worthy to be called your son; treat me like one of your hired hands."' So he set off and went to his father. But while he was still far off, his father saw him and was filled with compassion; he ran and put his arms around him and kissed him. Then the son said to him, 'Father, I have sinned against heaven and before you; I am no longer worthy to be called your son.' But the father said to his slaves, 'Quickly, bring out a robe—the best one—and put it on him; put a ring on his finger and sandals on his feet. And get the fatted calf and kill it, and let us eat and celebrate; for this son of

mine was dead and is alive again; he was lost and is found!' And they began to celebrate.

"Now his elder son was in the field; and when he came and approached the house, he heard music and dancing. He called one of the slaves and asked what was going on. He replied, 'Your brother has come, and your father has killed the fatted calf, because he has got him back safe and sound.' Then he became angry and refused to go in. His father came out and began to plead with him. But he answered his father, 'Listen! For all these years I have been working like a slave for you, and I have never disobeyed your command; yet you have never given me even a young goat so that I might celebrate with my friends. But when this son of yours came back, who has devoured your property with prostitutes, you killed the fatted calf for him!' Then the father said to him, 'Son, you are always with me, and all that is mine is yours. But we had to celebrate and rejoice, because this brother of yours was dead and has come to life; he was lost and has been found.'" (Luke 15:11-32)

What Jesus imaginatively conveys in this parable is that God's grace and forgiveness require no payment, no satisfaction. The prodigal son returns admitting that he is a sinner. Does the father ask for his accounting before he accepts him back? Does the father tell him that a price must be paid? Does the father act at all affronted by his son's dishonoring the family name by his "riotous living," as the King James Version so aptly puts it? No. The father asks nothing of him but runs out to meet him, puts his arms around him, and kisses him. The brother who stayed home and acted responsibly is the one troubled by his father's lack of demanding a price. For the other son thought his father *owed* him something because he had been faithful. Since his prodigal brother left and contributed nothing to the family while he was faithful to his father, he cried foul. It's the faithful son who thinks that justice hasn't been served by his father's free forgiveness. But the father isn't concerned about the justice of the situation; his only concern is his lost son, who now has been found.

This is a powerful parable and a potent image of God's grace. God's love is "pure" and "unbounded," in the words of that wonderful hymn by Charles Wesley, "Love Divine, All Loves Excelling." If we can come to see that the Word of God to us is a word of grace and acceptance, a word that overrides even our human sense of justice and fairness, then we can rethink some of the images of the atonement that have been passed down to us from our ancestors in the faith, putting them in their historical context and recognizing that the God Jesus imaged and spoke about doesn't require any sacrifice for us to be able to live within God's grace. In this passage and many others like it, the presented image of Jesus is an image of one who imagines God's grace to be wider than others had ever dreamed.

What is Jesus' significance for us today? Through the witness to him that we find in the New Testament, we learn to see the universality of God's grace. Through the narratives about him, comes the proclamation that God is love. In the words of the Gospel of John, in him we see the Father (John 14:9). As Christians, we confess that it is through this Jesus that meets us in the narratives of scripture and through the images of his living Spirit that are preached in the churches in our day and time that we come to know God and are able to live forgiven lives in an often unforgiving world. What Jesus does for us is to show us the way of God's grace, a grace present from the very beginning of God's creation. Jesus' death in itself does not bring about our reconciliation to God; it rather stands as a vivid re-presentation of the grace of God that is always and everywhere present (see Ogden 1982). Paul says it so well: "I am convinced that neither death, nor life, nor angels, nor rulers, nor things present, nor things to come, nor powers, nor height, nor depth, nor anything else in all creation, will be able to separate us from the love of God in Christ Jesus our Lord" (Romans 8:38-39). The significance of Jesus for us today is his showing us how to see the world as undergirded and graced by God's unfathomable love.

CHAPTER SIX

THINKING THROUGH TO GOD'S GRACE

I've argued in previous chapters that the growth of human knowledge about science, history, and the Bible makes it difficult for us to approach our faith in the ways that our forebears did. Moreover, the very notion that God creates the world in a constantly unfolding process suggests that we are called in faith to understand ourselves as created in and for *this* time and *this* place, and that we must use the best thinking available today as we seek to understand ourselves, our world, and our God. Christian faith was not fully given in the first century; Christians' faith was decisively shaped then, but grows and changes as Christians live in different times and cultures.

In chapter 4 we saw that our consciousness of history and its relation to human thought means that we must develop new understandings of the Bible and its functions in Christian communities of faith. The Bible is a thoroughly human book that arose in human history. Its contents are interwoven with the ideas and images of the cultures out of which it arose. Many of us can no longer think that the Bible gives us a direct revelation of God, as if the words of the Bible were the words of God. Rather, we must understand the Bible as the Word of God in that we discern in those words from the past, glimmerings of insight into God, as the authors of scripture came to view and understand God.

99

In chapter 5 we examined the implications of the new view of scripture on our view of Jesus Christ. New understandings of the Bible complicate both orthodoxy and the older liberalism, for both views are implicitly based on the historical validity of the New Testament. For orthodoxy, the New Testament's report on Jesus is true in all aspects. Jesus' teachings, his healings, his miracles, his resurrection—all occurred as described in the Bible. The older liberalism, while accepting the results of biblical scholarship that questioned the supernaturalistic and miraculous elements in scripture, nonetheless thought it possible, using the tools of historical research developed in the nineteenth century, to winnow the "kernels" of historically true events from the "husks" of the early church's interpretative accretions in order to find the "real" historical Jesus, who preached and taught about "the brotherhood of man under the fatherhood of God" (see, for example, Harnack 1957). But as critics of nineteenth-century liberalism showed, what the liberals ended up seeing as actually historical in Jesus were precisely those characteristics that best fit their own religious worldview. What they found in the historical Jesus was quite often what they unconsciously wanted to find in him. The modern consensus of most biblical scholars is that a full reconstruction of the Jesus of history is not possible. Moreover, what can be said about Jesus with historical probability is far too meager to support the traditional christological claims. We must rethink the significance of the biblical pictures of Jesus so that we recognize that our faith is based, as indeed the faith of Christians throughout the ages has been, on the biblical images of Jesus and not on some historical figure that lies deeply embedded beneath the layers of interpretation and preaching that constitute our New Testament.

Recognizing that we cannot get beyond the biblical pictures of Jesus, we must come to a new appreciation of the evolution in religious thought that is represented by the earliest churches' preaching about Jesus. This is the content of the New Testament. This is what ignited the growth of Christianity. This is what continues to inspire Christians today. Though we recognize its symbolic and mythic characterizations of Jesus, we can come to an appreciation of the new way of thinking about God that is enveloped by the gospels, by Paul's letters, and by the other New Testament writings. The truth of the gospel proclamation is not a result of the accuracy of the New Testament's history: it is the result of the truth that comes into being through and in that gospel proclamation: the truth that God is gracious and that to live a life recognizing and responding to that grace is to be redeemed.

Now it is time to turn to that most central idea in Christians' faith, the idea of God. How can we think about God today, if indeed what has been argued to this point so undercuts traditional approaches to Christians' faith?

THE LANGUAGE OF FAITH

Words function for us in many ways. Often, we think of words simply as labels for things in our world. When we say, "The coffee cup is on the table," we interpret this to mean that there are two physical objects, related to one another in such a way that one is on top of the other. These words are tags that language uses to represent or mirror the objects "out there." Children learn this function of language first; such a view, which philosophers call "naive realism," serves us well in our everyday life. When I'm driving and my wife calls out, "Watch out for that car!" I look for the thing out there in physical reality that I need to avoid hitting.

But not all words function so simply. In fact, we move away from the idea that words "tag" physical realities as soon as we use words to represent categories of physical objects rather than physical objects themselves. For example, if I ask, "Does anyone in the room have a coffee cup?" I no longer use "coffee cup" as a tag or label for a particular physical object. In fact, I don't even have the precise object I'm looking for directly in mind. Someone may answer "Yes" because she holds a green-striped handleless cardboard cup, but it is very unlikely that an image of such a cup was in my mind as I asked the question. Yet when she offers it to me, I immediately see that she has answered my question accurately, and others in the room would concur. Even in our everyday experience, words do not always function as simple labels that directly map discrete physical objects.

As we move from words that relate to concrete physical objects to words that have to do with human life and experience, the model of naive realism breaks down even further. Words that are part and parcel of human experience—words like love, hate, freedom, oppression, family, country, faith—are not amenable to an approach that looks for some physical reality "out there" to which these "labels" apply. Certainly these words include physical dimensions: my wife and three daughters physically live in the same home and my daughters could be physically identified through DNA testing to be my genetic descendants. But when we talk of "family" we mean more than physical living arrangements or genetic continuities. The concern about the breakdown of the family so often voiced in our society really has to do with a whole complex of issues that relate to values that transcend empirical description or formulation. A similar point can be made about the referent, the physical reality, to which the label "The United States of America" applies. What, exactly, is "it" to which we pledge allegiance when we stand with our hands over our hearts at public functions? Surely it is not simply a physical geographical expanse, nor is it the sum total of living persons within those geographical boundaries, nor is it even a piece of paper called the Constitution housed in a hermetically sealed display case in the National Archives. The United States of America is fundamentally an idea, not a thing, and for us to understand what loyalty and patriotism are we must recognize that we are dealing with a reality quite different from physical reality.

This should be no startling news for those who have participated in Christian churches. I remember as a child being told again and again that the church is not the building but the people. But even that doesn't fully encompass the truth, for the church is not simply a congregation of people either. The church, like "The United States of America," is an idea that encompasses many dimensions, none of which can be reduced to a single referent out there in the empirically experienced world.

So it is the case with many of the words we use as Christians in our faith, worship, and study. "Salvation," "sin," "grace," "heaven," "Christ," and the like are words more akin to "United States of America" or "justice" than to "coffee cup." These words don't simply point to "things" out there; they shape and constitute the realities of which they speak. Moreover, the words of faith are interwoven. The concept of "salvation" is shaped and influenced by our concepts of "grace," "Christ," and "sin." So as we explore the language that constitutes Christians' faith, we must always look at the way the main ideas that constitute that faith relate to one another and to ideas present in the ethos of contemporary culture. Though all language constitutes our world and experience to some degree, the degree to which our religious language constitutes our religious world is very high—so high, in fact, that the realities of faith are often spoken of as "hidden" or "unknowable" apart from faith.[1]

The idea of God is the keystone in a Christian's religious world. Other ideas may be foundational, for instance, the idea of Christ, but it is the idea of God that finally holds together all the other ideas in the believer's understanding. That's why it's so important for us to think seriously about the notions of God that we hold: Without an adequate conception of God, the archway of Christian faith falls to the ground; with an adequate conception, the archway provides an entryway into a viable way of faith for Christians today.

Our Idea of God

I've emphasized that religious language is constitutive of faith and that the keystone idea within Christians' faith is "God." For

---

1. One thinks here of John Calvin's claim in his *Institutes of the Christian Religion* that piety is the true requisite for knowledge of God (I.ii.1).

many Christians, this will be saying far too little of God's external reality. After all, our tradition claims that "God" *does* function as a name for a specific object, not one experienced physically like coffee cups and trees but one given to us through revelation and spiritual experience. I want to address why I think these approaches are by themselves inadequate.[2]

Prior to the late–nineteenth century, Christians for the most part did not ask questions about their foundational assumption that the Bible contained unique communications from God to humankind. Although the terms "biblical literalism" and "biblical inerrancy" are actually the products of reactions to the late-nineteenth-century developments, it's fair to say that in general our forebears in Christian faith believed that the scriptures were uniquely revealed and inspired by God; therefore, they could be taken at face value. When the prophets say, "Thus says the Lord," the words that follow are God's words; when the gospels say, "Jesus said," what follows are the words of Jesus. With the further identification of Jesus with God in the early church, Christians for centuries were able to assume that the referent for "God" was self-disclosed in these sacred texts.

For many Christians this view is no longer tenable. As we saw in chapter 4, critical-historical analyses of Christian scripture have forever undercut the older assumptions. As a document arising in the ancient Near Eastern and Hellenistic worlds, the Bible's views of God are themselves deeply colored by ancient Israelite and Hellenistic patterns of thought. The Bible does not give us God or God's words in an unambiguous way. It gives us ways ancient Israelites and early Christians thought and spoke about God—ways that are foundational for our own thinking but not ways that can be accepted lock, stock, and barrel. Hence, historical studies in this century have led most biblical scholars to move away from the view that the Bible contains directly revealed words and deeds of God. And Christians must

---

2. Much of the following discussion depends on the work of Gordon Kaufman (1981, 1993, 1996).

take these new views seriously as we try to think through to God in our day.

The existence of other world religions also makes a simple appeal to revelation as sufficient for our thinking about God difficult. We today understand other world religions to a degree unparalleled in the history of Christianity. Because of our shrinking world, in which instant communications and rapid travel make distant cultures accessible and familiar, we often come to know other religions through knowing persons who are adherents to those other religions. We see that persons of other faiths are human beings just like us, with similar fears and hopes. Whereas our forebears found it easy from a distance to think of other religions as worthy of condemnation and even violent suppression, we can no longer think in such terms. Christians today explore other world religions on those religions' own terms to understand them, not simply to devise arguments against those religions as a way of bolstering Christianity.

A result of this new appreciation of other religions has been the recognition that appeals to revelation are part and parcel of many religious traditions in addition to Christianity. The sorts of arguments made concerning the validity of revelation in the Christian scripture are mirrored in approaches to the Qur'an in Islam and the Torah in Judaism. All such arguments tend to be based internally on the circular self-validating character of the revelation: we know God through revelation and we know that the scripture is revelation because it is revealed of God. Within each religion such arguments seem cogent and plausible. But when we look at such claims comparatively across religious traditions, we realize that the same sorts of internal, self-validating claims are made by most traditions. What's good for the goose is good for the gander: if Christians rely on internal, self-validating arguments from within our scripture to establish the objectivity of God, so also must we allow participants in other religious traditions to do the same. Precisely by trying to show the human origins and mythic character of other religions' claims to revelation, we've come to recognize the human and mythic character of our own. We cannot today simply appeal to the authority of biblical revelation to establish the reality and character of the God who stands behind the biblical images and stories, because we've come to know too much about their origins and the origins of all religious scriptures to make such a view viable in our world.

But many would argue that biblical revelation is a record of the prophets' *experiences* with God and is hence just a particular instance of a larger phenomenon that does give us the object to which our religious terms apply. The phenomenon of religious experience for many is the key for understanding God. "God" is the tag for the object of that experience.

There's great appeal in this approach today. We live in a world in which science proceeds by testing its claims against sensory experience, and the authority of individual experience is primary in our thinking. We don't trust authorities as our forebears did; we often won't believe something until we've experienced it ourselves. For many, this appeal to sensory experience is paralleled in the appeal to religious experience. Just as sensory experience leads us to knowledge about the objects of sensory experience, religious experience leads us to knowledge about the objects of religious experience.

Such religious or spiritual experience is categorically different from sensory experience and typically depends on a dualistic view of human life and experience that separates the spiritual from the physical. Ironically, the dualistic view on which this distinction is predicated is itself a product of the modern world in its philosophical foundations. Although this sort of physical-spiritual dualism has its antecedents in our cultural thought going back to the Greeks, especially in Plato and the Platonists, it was René Descartes (1596–1650) who solidified the separation between the mental world and the physical world that enabled natural science to develop on its own without conflicting with the religious beliefs of most European intellectuals. In this view science has to do with the physical world and religion with the spiritual. Religious or spiritual experiences are indicative of a nonphysical world present in parallel with the physical world, and experiences in this spiritual world are valid as indicators of the spiritual realities to which the religious terms point, as empirical experiences are indicators of the physical world.

But an important difference between religious experience and sensory experience causes the parallelism to break down. Whereas science is predicated on publicly observable phenomena that can be commonly experienced, religious experience typically is subjective and individual. Let's go back to the coffee cup we spoke of earlier. Imagine a group of us in a classroom together. I set an object on a table in our midst. I ask you, "What is this object?" Without hesitation, all answer, "A coffee cup." I ask for further description and am given details about size, shape, color, and the like. Should someone disagree with the others about the size, we could conduct an "experiment" to check out the conflicting observations. A quick check with a ruler would show that the coffee cup is four inches tall, not six as the dissident suggests. At this point, should the dissident not concede his mistake and continue to hold that the cup is six inches tall in spite of the common perceptions of the rest of the group, we would hardly know what to do. But surely the discussion would turn away from the coffee cup to the dissident. For now the question would become either, "What is wrong with him? Is he crazy? On drugs? Does he need new glasses?" or "Why is he lying to us? What is he trying to gain by saying something that he knows is not true?"

Should we gather the same group to talk about God, a very important fundamental difference emerges: we cannot put God before us on the table! Hence, our ability to talk about experiences that we have of God *in common*, is of a different character from the way we talk about common experiences of coffee cups or other empirical objects. Indeed, internal sensations offer a better analogy to religious experience than perceptions of external objects.

Let's use our same group to assess this. Suppose this time I ask the group to describe hunger. We cannot place "hunger" on the table before us, because, unlike coffee cups, hunger is not an external object. But suppose further that I ask the group to fast for two days before our meeting. After two days I suspect all will have experienced hunger. Should we then try to describe our experiences of hunger, we would find many common identifiable traits: a growling abdomen, a general weakness, an intense desire to find food, and the like. We could discuss traits and determine the common features in our experiences of hunger, but we do not really experience hunger as a common experience in the ways that we commonly experience external sensory objects. Because it is internal, the "object" to which we give the name "hunger" is intensely private in that it is an experience internal to me, not experientially available to others as *my* experience, although they may have had similar internal experiences themselves, which makes it possible for us to talk about hunger.[3]

But what if a dissident appears and describes her experience of hunger quite differently, indeed disagrees that she ever had the internal sensations of growling, of weakness, of desire for food, that the rest of us report. Can we say, "No, you're wrong, you do have those sensations"? Of course not. Since the object of our discussion is not publicly before us but is rather a private experience, we cannot find a ruler as before to measure the disagreement so as to judge between descriptions. We might even question whether the dissident had really fasted for two days, but we also know that people often experience hunger in different ways and can give different descriptions of it. My point here is

---

3. Men typically find themselves unable to enter fully into a conversation among women who have experienced labor and childbirth. Although fathers today are often present during labor and delivery, they do not experience childbirth internally as do women. So two mothers will be able to speak of the commonalities in their individual experiences of pregnancy and childbirth in ways unavailable to their respective husbands, who were, however, actually present with their wives during labor and delivery but unable to participate in the internal experience of birth.

that with regard to internal sensations, what we mean by "common experience" is rather different from what we mean by that term when speaking of external observable experiences that underlie natural science.

Let's carry this example even one step further. What if we gathered together a group comprising persons of different religious traditions, and the question was not about hunger but about their religious experiences? In the group are Christian, Jew, Muslim, Buddhist, Sikh, Hindu, and others. Let's also assume that they can communicate in a common language. If I were to ask them to describe their experiences of God, only some would even know what I was asking, for "God" is a term that is tied to particular ways of conceiving what we take to be ultimate in reality. Suppose I asked instead that each describe his or her particular religious experiences of whatever is central in his or her own tradition. Though more might know what I was asking, the answers they offer would be as diverse as the traditions they represent. In fact, it would be difficult to find anything in their outwardly divergent descriptions that would lead us to believe that they had had internal experiences of a common reality at all.

Friedrich Schleiermacher (1768–1834) developed his whole approach to religion and Christianity as a way of preserving the notion of a common human religious experience in the face of the outward differences in religious expressions. For Schleiermacher, Christian doctrines are but attempts to bring to expression a fundamental "feeling of absolute dependence" that underlies all human experience. God is not an "object" of knowledge or a presupposition of the moral life, as God was for Immanuel Kant. "God," for Schleiermacher, is the designation for "the *Whence* of our receptive and active existence as implied in this self-consciousness [of absolute dependence]" (1963, 16). God is known only indirectly as the source of the immediate feeling of dependence.

What was very new in Schleiermacher's approach was that he identified religious experience as underlying all of our experiences. Rather than being an experience that we sometimes have and sometimes don't, religious feeling is always operative in us. In this sense my hunger example fails to convey Schleiermacher's idea. He himself appeals to the notion of our self-consciousness as a way of trying to identify the experience on which religion is based. Just as we are implicitly self-conscious when we are conscious of external things and internal sensations, so we also implicitly experience absolute dependence in all our doing, acting, and feeling. This experience is not one experience of a particular religious object; it is the implicit experience of dependence that is part and parcel of every experience we have.

Once we bring this implicit underlying self-consciousness of absolute dependence to a level of explicit attention, says Schleiermacher, we become dependent on images and stories available to us in our culture to talk about and think about this noncognitive experience of dependence. Christians speak about this feeling in terms of Jesus Christ and the images and symbols that have arisen in Christianity to articulate this deep experience. But other religions have their own symbols and vocabularies to express this sense of absolute dependence. Schleiermacher is important in the history of Christian theology precisely because he laid out a way of thinking about religion that enabled Christians to see other world religions as attempts to express in their own stories and symbols the truth that Christians talked about through theirs. But for him all human experience was undergirded by the sense of absolute dependence; all humans could bring this fundamental human experience to expression, even if the forms of the expression varied from culture to culture. Though Schleiermacher gave arguments why Christianity was the highest form of religious tradition (based on its being most adequate to express the contents of the consciousness of being absolutely dependent), his recognition that Christian language about God was fundamentally based on experience rather than on revelation was the spark that ignited the development of liberal Christian theology in the nineteenth and twentieth centuries.

But even Schleiermacher's attempt to point to the referent of "God" indirectly by means of common human experience has its problems. First, how does one talk about a discrete experience when the experience in question is not "an" experience at all but is more a dimension present in all experience? Indeed, Schleiermacher claims that such an experience, once we reflect upon it, flees from our immediate consciousness when we try to objectify it by making it an object of thought. Many of Schleiermacher's critics have pointed to the difficulty of knowing just what a "common" experience is in situations when people are not usually intuitively aware of it.

Second, a more telling objection arises out of the very historicism that we've seen to be an important part of the intellectual world of the twentieth century. Does it make sense to make such a "clean" distinction between experience and thought as is presupposed in Schleiermacher's approach? Is it really the case that we have raw, uninterpreted religious experience, which then comes to expression in differing ways, resulting in the different world religions? Many philosophers today question this assumption, which has been part of Western thought for centuries. And this is the case even in the philosophy of science. Even our sensory observations are not totally independent of our language and thought. As philosophers of science express it, all observation is "theory-laden" and hence the language we use arises out of our theories and shapes even our most basic empirical experiences (Kuhn 1970; Toulmin 1972; Berstein 1983).

Since language and ideas actually shape our experience, using experience to find the definitive references for our religious language ends up finding objects that look much like the ideas and images contained within the traditions out of which the exploration begins. Even in mystical experience, the form of religious experience that supposedly is most direct and least subject to interpretative distortion, we find that Christians have mystical experiences of a decidedly Christian slant; Muslims, of an Islamic slant; and Buddhists, of a Buddhist slant. Though, as William James showed (1961), certain commonalities can be found among mystical experiences, nevertheless the contents of such experience seem always to evolve out of the religious categories and ideas brought to the experience rather than arising purely out of the experience itself (Proudfoot 1985).

We have therefore no direct unmediated experience of God, only experiences deeply shaped and constituted by our religious template of ideas and images. God's ultimate and final reality stands as a mystery before us. We can know and experience God only insofar as we do so through the ideas and images of our traditions. Yet those traditions, we must realize, are themselves products of human culture. We cannot get behind those traditions to see what God is really like because the notion of God is itself a part of those traditions.

In this sense theology is much like a great cathedral. A great medieval cathedral is surely a work of human design and construction. The way such a cathedral comes to shape the experiences of those who worship there with its grandeur and majesty plays a fundamental role in their religious life. But no one would confuse this cathedral of human construction directly with God. We might say that the cathedral points to God, expresses the majesty and grandeur of God, and enables us to experience God, but surely the cathedral is not built by God nor does it directly link us to God. So also is it the case with our theology. The ideas and images that have evolved in Christian faith are surely products of human culture and history. Like the cathedral, our theological concepts have a discoverable history. They came about in the midst of human history and, as we now more clearly see, were honed in conflict and controversy in Christianity's development. Yet like the cathedral, they can still function for us to shape a religious world worthy of our commitment and loyalty. "God" is one of the greatest ideas to evolve in human culture. And the particularly Christian idea of God fundamentally shapes the way many of us see ourselves and our world. How can we recognize that our idea of God is *our* idea of God and yet live before life's profound mystery in faith and trust, allowing the reality of that idea to shape our every thought and action?

God is an idea. And for believers, God is real. But these two claims aren't mutually exclusive, for many of the realities most important to us as humans are present to us as ideas and not as empirical realities. Indeed, in this sense many of the most important realities for us are *spiritual*. However we approach God religiously, we must recognize that theologically God is first and foremost an idea. Apart from some idea of God there is no experience of God. And different ideas of God lead to different experiences of God.

I use the word "idea" here in a very broad sense to include not only concepts but also images. As members of the primate order, we descended from animal ancestors for whom sight was the primary sense. When we think about things, we therefore often employ visual images; we "picture" things in our minds. Often these mental pictures are the first ideas we have as children, and they continue to play crucial roles in our mature adult thinking.

For instance, think about God right now. Most people will report that they have some visual image in mind when they think about God. Those images undoubtedly arise from our memory of paintings to which we were early exposed, or, in my case, the illustrations in my first Bible. If you are of more abstract and philosophical inclination, you might envision pure whiteness or a perfect circle. However we picture God in our imagination, our earliest and most persistent ideas of God tend to involve visual images.

Our human ability to imagine God, through abstract thought and mental images, is the source both of our most sublime religious inspirations and our most narrow religious bigotries. In ancient Israel, there were clear prohibitions against the making of "graven images" of God.[4] Such images would inevitably result

---

4. Exodus 20:4. I preserve here the translation "graven image" from the RSV rather than the NRSV's "idol" for reasons that subsequently will become apparent.

in false worship, because no graven image could represent God. We should realize that the prohibition against idolatry in the Old Testament needs to be recast in light of what we now know of the sources and origins of our religious images: the prohibition against "graven images" needs to extend to "mental images." When we mistakenly take our *idea* of God to be identical with God's transcendent reality, we, like our Israelite forebears, commit idolatry.

Examples of such idolatry abound in history. But I choose an example that causes many disagreements within our present churches: the idea of God as male. Think again of the idea of God you had a moment ago. I suspect that many of us who imagined a person imaged a male person, a man. Our Christian forebears' identification of Jesus with God causes us special difficulty with our images. Since Jesus is male, and Jesus is God, then God is male. But ponder for just a moment what it means to be male or female. Maleness and femaleness are part of our, as well as much of the rest of the organic world's, created nature. Sexual differentiation serves a very important function in the natural world, and strange as it may sound, that function is not primarily reproductive. Were reproduction the only goal, asexual reproduction would be much more efficient. Sexual reproduction evolved, however, to enable diversity to become part of the reproductive process. Variations that arise from and are passed on by sexual reproduction are the building blocks of evolution and hence of the increasing levels of complexity that finally resulted in human beings. Sexual distinction is therefore part and parcel of our created nature, or, as theologians prefer to say, our finitude. At the species level, males aren't much good apart from females and females aren't much good apart from males. As a species, *Homo sapiens* is male and female, and this differentiation is essential.

But of course it is also limiting for individuals within the species. As a male or a female we are incomplete without the opposite. No matter what our culture tells us about individuals' independence, gender roles, and sexual equality, sexual differentiation is a limitation of our created nature.

What happens when we confuse our male image of God with the reality to which our idea points? We think that God really *is* male; we attribute a characteristic of our finitude to ultimate reality. This, I suggest, is a particularly modern form of idolatry. We make our particular finite ideas of God into "graven images," graven in our minds and on our hearts rather than on stone or wood, but graven nonetheless.

But that leaves us in a peculiarly difficult situation: we recognize that all our thinking about God is *our* thinking, and yet how else can we think about ultimate reality? And here it seems to me we must recognize a fundamental circularity in our thinking about our faith. God stands beyond our every concept and idea and image. Yet precisely in faith we come to God, worship God, and experience God through this complex of ideas that we've inherited from our forebears in the faith. Without the symbols, images, and ideas faith is but an empty shell, a longing for the infinite without a way to give content to that infinite. And yet, whatever content we give to the ultimate, it is always our construction. We, like Solomon, set out to build a house for God. Just as the people of Judah believed that God really dwelt in the Temple and was located there, we begin to think that God really is like our ideas of God. Just as the people of Judah learned that God was beyond the Temple after its destruction, so too we must continually learn that God is beyond our every attempt to think about God through our finite ideas. As H. R. Niebuhr puts it, "None is absolute save God and ... the absolutizing of anything finite is ruinous to the finite itself" (1960, 113). And Niebuhr's warning must surely extend to our very ideas of God, which are themselves finite and most liable to absolutizing.

The recognition that our theological ideas are human constructs not written in the heavens is humbling. We cannot be as cocksure as our forebears that our view of ultimate reality is the one and only correct view. And we are brought to see the pretensions of many of our faith claims when we act as though we are the exclusive spokesmen and spokeswomen for God. And yet, especially in the classic form of theological reflection known as the *via negativa*, there have always been Christians who have recognized that God's reality cannot be directly stated but can only be "talked around," if you will. As a result, Christian faith must today be more willing to rely on a confessional method of reflection: stating what we believe and how we think of God's reality while recognizing that others see things differently and that none of our views can be presently adjudicated by direct appeal to that reality.

But we must also honestly admit that recognizing the constructive character of our theology can debilitate. For those for whom certainty is a prerequisite to conviction and commitment, this way of seeing faith and theology will be destructive, for it undercuts the classic orthodox assumption that the truths of faith have been handed directly to us from God. Let me be as clear on this as I can be: what we have in the varieties of Christians' faith are worldviews that arose and evolved in human cultures through past centuries; worldviews that no doubt seek to describe and set the context for relating to ultimate reality, but human worldviews nonetheless. For many, this will be going too far and I deeply respect their disagreement. All I can do is set forth the conclusions that I and many other Christians have reached after having looked carefully at these issues, taking completely seriously what we've learned over the past centuries about religion, science, history, and culture.

And yet the recognition of theology's constructive character is also liberating. For in recognizing the constructive character of our theology, we need not be bound by the inadequate formulations of our forebears; formulations that often have been the justification for great suffering, persecution, and oppression even within the life of faith. What it means, for instance, for us to take seriously that maleness is not an inherent characteristic of God is that our religious structures—both institutional and conceptual—can be reformed to be more inclusive. Liberating the notion of God's creative activity from the model most often used within Christian history to describe that creative activity—namely the model of human crafting of artifacts—enables us to talk meaningfully again about God's creativeness without becoming trapped in a supernaturalistic creationism. Freeing the idea of God from the anthropomorphic mythology that surrounds it in the Bible frees us from the cosmic egocentricity of thinking that we human beings are the real meaning and end of this universe. In short, we are brought to realize that our ultimate justification as human beings cannot reside in any of our ideologies but finally rests in that which utterly transcends us. This is liberating; indeed, this is knowledge of salvation. Our forebears in Christian faith discovered this key insight. Indeed, it's precisely the image Jesus paints of God's reality. His later followers spoke of it in these terms: we live by God's grace and by God's grace alone. Hence we're brought back full circle to an essential truth that underlies the gospel story. That is, after all, where Christian faith must begin. We cannot escape that circularity. And yet we must be fully conscious of it if we are to live faithfully in the midst of our world today.

To live as a Christian is to imagine life in the context of God's grace. It is to see ourselves and all that befalls us as finally within an ultimate context of acceptance, forgiveness, and love. It is a way of seeing and a way of being that one must adopt; it is not something that can be read off the sensory world. Ultimately, we must commit our lives to this way of seeing. Only then will we experience the spiritual reality of God.

I've argued in this book that Christians ought to apply the very best thinking available when we think about our faith. Such thinking, I argued, shows us that many of the assumptions made by our forebears about the Bible, Jesus, and God must be reevaluated in the light of the times and places in which they lived as those contrast to the times and places in which we live. But such thinking also enables us to see, through our ancestors' witnesses to God's reality, the present reality of God's grace. Through their witness, as that witness is refined and reforged on the anvils of current thought, we come to think about God anew. And in the very process of thinking through the ideas and images of God, we experience God's reality as grace. For Christians, the ultimate mystery that stands as the very source and being of the universe and all within it finally boils down to grace. We live in God's grace. That's the essential meaning and message of Christian faith.

There are other ways to understand Christian faith. I do not claim that my emphasis on grace as foundational for a Christian way of thinking is the only way one can think about Christian faith. But it is *a* way, and one not inconsistent with the ways of our ancestors. It is an option for contemporary Christians to think about our faith. That's why I've emphasized that Christian faith is not a set of doctrines, or a collection of creeds, or a body of propositions to be given assent. Rather faith is always our human attitude toward and our relation to the mystery we call ultimate reality. What is really important is not Christian faith, but Christians' faith. As a result, Christians' faith will always be multiform and plural in expression. For those of us for whom the intellect is an essential component in our approach to life, there will always be an important place for thinking about our faith. My hope is that I've shown that such thinking need not lead away from a living faith but can itself lead us to imagine and hence experience God's grace in our day.

Anselm. 1958. *St. Anselm: Proslogium; Monologium; An Appendix in Behalf of the Fool by Gaunilon; and Cur Deus Homo*. Translated by Sidney Norton Deane. Reprint ed. Philosophical Classics. La Salle, Ill.: Open Court Publishing Co.

Ayer, Alfred Jules. 1952. *Language, Truth and Logic*. New York: Dover Publications.

Berstein, Richard J. 1983. *Beyond Objectivism and Relativism: Science, Hermeneutics, and Praxis*. Philadelphia: University of Pennsylvania Press.

Bowler, Peter J. 1989. *Evolution: The History of an Idea*. Revised ed. Berkeley: University of California Press.

Bultmann, Rudolf. 1958. *Jesus Christ and Mythology*. New York: Charles Scribner's Sons.

―――. 1984. *The New Testament and Mythology and Other Basic Writings*. Edited and translated by Schubert M. Ogden. Philadelphia: Fortress Press.

Calvin, John. 1960. *Calvin: Institutes of the Christian Religion*. Translated by Ford Lewis Battles. 2 vols. Library of Christian Classics. Philadelphia: Westminster Press.

Collingwood, R. G. 1993. *The Idea of History*. Edited by Jan van der Dussen. Revised ed. Oxford: Oxford University Press.

Collins, John J. 1995. *The Scepter and the Star: The Messiahs of the Dead Sea Scrolls and Other Ancient Literature*. The Anchor Bible Reference Library. New York: Doubleday.

Collins, Raymond F. 1988. *Letters That Paul Did Not Write: The Epistle to the Hebrews and the Pauline Pseudepigrapha*. Good News Studies, vol. 28. Wilmington, Del.: Michael Glazier.

Daly, Mary. 1984. *Pure Lust: Elemental Feminist Philosophy*. Boston: Beacon Press.

Darwin, Charles. 1950. *The Origin of Species by Means of Natural Selection and The Descent of Man*. The Modern Library of the World's Best Books. New York: Modern Library.

Descartes, René. 1968. *Discourse on Method and the Meditations*. Translated by F. E. Sutcliffe. Penguin Classics. New York: Penguin Books.

Finocchiaro, Maurice A., ed. 1989. *The Galileo Affair: A Documentary History*. California Studies in the History of Science. Berkeley: University of California Press.

Friedman, Richard Elliott. 1987. *Who Wrote the Bible?* New York: Summit Books.

Funk, Robert W., Roy W. Hoover, and The Jesus Seminar. 1993. *The Five Gospels: The Search for the Authentic Words of Jesus*. New York: Macmillan, Polebridge Press.

Grant, Edward. 1978. "Cosmology." In *Science in the Middle Ages*, edited by David C. Lindberg. Chicago: University of Chicago Press.

Harnack, Adolf. 1957. *What Is Christianity?* Translated by Thomas Bailey Saunders. New York: Harper and Row, Harper Torchbooks.

Hobbes, Thomas. 1962. *Leviathan, or the Matter, Forme and Power of a Commonwealth Ecclessiasticall and Civil*. Edited by Michael Oakeshott. New York: Collier Books.

James, William. 1961. *The Varieties of Religious Experience*. New York: Collier Macmillan Books.

Johnson, Elizabeth A. 1994. *She Who Is: The Mystery of God in Feminist Theological Discourse*. New York: Crossroad.

Jowett, Benjamin. 1860. "On the Interpretation of Scripture." In *Essays and Reviews*. London: John W. Parker and Son.

Kant, Immanuel. 1957. *On History*. Translated by Lewis White Beck, Robert E. Anchor, and Emil L. Fackenheim. Edited by Lewis White Beck. Indianapolis: Bobbs-Merrill Co.

Kaufman, Gordon D. 1981. *The Theological Imagination: Constructing the Concept of God*. Philadelphia: Westminster Press.

———. 1993. *In Face of Mystery: A Constructive Theology*. Cambridge, Mass.: Harvard University Press.

———. 1996. *God, Mystery, Diversity*. Minneapolis: Fortress Press.

Kee, Howard Clark. 1990. *What Can We Know About Jesus?* Understanding Jesus Today Series. Cambridge: Cambridge University Press.

Kuhn, Thomas S. 1970. *The Structure of Scientific Revolutions*. Edited by Otto Neurath. 2nd, enlarged ed. International Encyclopedia of Unified Science Series, vol. 2, no. 2. Chicago: University of Chicago Press.

Lerner, Gerda. 1986. *The Creation of Patriarchy*. Women and History, vol. 1. New York: Oxford University Press.

Lloyd, G. E. R. 1970. *Early Greek Science: Thales to Aristotle*. Ancient Culture and Society. New York: W. W. Norton and Co.

Locke, John. 1975. *An Essay Concerning Human Understanding*. Edited by P. H. Nidditch. The Clarendon Edition of the Works of John Locke. Oxford: Clarendon Press.

Luther, Martin. 1958. *Luther's Commentary on Genesis*. Translated by J. Theodore Mueller. 2 vols. Grand Rapids, Mich.: Zondervan.

Meier, John P. 1991– . *A Marginal Jew: Rethinking the Historical Jesus*. 3 vols. Anchor Bible Reference Library. New York: Doubleday.

Newton, Isaac. 1934. *Sir Isaac Newton's Mathematical Principles of Natural Philosophy and His System of the World*. Translated by Andrew Mott. Edited by Florian Cajori. Berkeley, Calif.: University of California Press.

Niebuhr, H. Richard. 1941. *The Meaning of Revelation*. New York: Macmillan Publishing Co.

———. 1960. *Radical Monotheism and Western Culture: With Supplementary Essays*. New York: Harper and Row.

Ogden, Schubert M. 1982. *The Point of Christology*. San Francisco: Harper and Row.

O'Neill, J. C. 1992. "Biblical Criticism." In *The Anchor Bible Dictionary*, edited by David Noel Freedman. 6 vols. New York: Doubleday.

Paley, William. 1810–12. *The Works of William Paley in Five Volumes*. 5 vols. Boston: Joshua Belcher.

Passmore, John. 1967. "Logical Positivism." In *The Encyclopedia of Philosophy*, edited by Paul Edwards. 5 vols. New York: Macmillan.

Pedersen, Olaf. 1991. *Galileo and the Council of Trent*. New ed. Studi Galileiani, vol. 1, no. 6. Vatican Observatory Publications, Special Series. Vatican City: Specola Vaticana.

Pelikan, Jaroslav. 1971–89. *The Christian Tradition: A History of the Development of Doctrine*. 5 vols. Chicago: University of Chicago Press.

Plantinga, Alvin. 1983. "Reason and Belief in God." In *Faith and Rationality: Reason and Belief in God*, edited by Alvin Plantinga and Nicholas Wolterstorff. Notre Dame, Ind.: University of Notre Dame Press.

Plato. 1961. *The Collected Dialogues of Plato Including the Letters*. Translated by Lane Cooper et al. Edited by Edith Hamilton and Huntington Cairns. Princeton, N.J.: Princeton University Press.

Proudfoot, Wayne. 1985. *Religious Experience*. Berkeley: University of California Press.

Rorty, Richard. 1979. *Philosophy and the Mirror of Nature*. Princeton, N.J.: Princeton University Press.

Schleiermacher, Friedrich. 1958. *On Religion: Speeches to Its Cultured Despisers*. New York: Harper and Row.

————. 1963. *The Christian Faith*. Translated by H. R. MacKintosh and J. S. Stewart. 2 vols. New York: Harper and Row, Harper Torchbooks.

Schüssler Fiorenza, Elisabeth. 1983. *In Memory of Her: A Feminist Theological Reconstruction of Christian Origins*. New York: Crossroad.

Schweitzer, Albert. 1968. *The Quest of the Historical Jesus: A Critical Study of Its Progress from Reimarus to Wrede*. Translated by W. Montgomery. New York: Macmillan Publishing Co.

Spinoza, Benedict de. 1951. *The Chief Works of Benedict de Spinoza*. Translated by R. H. M. Elwes. 2 vols. New York: Dover.

Tillich, Paul. 1967. *Systematic Theology: Three Volumes in One*. Chicago: University of Chicago Press.

Toulmin, Stephen. 1972. *Human Understanding: The Collective Use and Evolution of Concepts*. Princeton, N.J.: Princeton University Press.

————. 1990. *Cosmopolis: The Hidden Agenda of Modernity*. New York: Free Press.

Tracy, David. 1987. *Plurality and Ambiguity: Hermeneutics, Religion, Hope*. San Francisco: Harper and Row.

————. 1994. "Theology and the Many Faces of Modernity." *Theology Today* 51/1:104-14.

Troeltsch, Ernst. 1991. "Historical and Dogmatic Methods in Theology." In *Religion in History*, translated by James Luther Adams and Walter F. Bense. Minneapolis: Fortress Press.

Weinberg, Steven. 1988. *The First Three Minutes: A Modern View of the Origin of the Universe*. Updated ed. New York: Basic Books.

Eusebius, 19
evil, 78
evolution, 41, 44
existential significance, human, 86
experience: common human, 107-9, 111; religious, 106; sensory, 29, 106, 111

faith, religious, 85
feeling of absolute dependence, 109-10
feminist thought, 56
First Amendment, 45
fundamentalism, 69, 80, 84

Galatians, Letter to the, 87
Galelei, Galileo, 36-37, 46
Galen, 50
Genesis, book of, 45, 46
God: creative activity of, 45; as creator, 38; direct experience of, 112; as good, 72; as idea, 103-4, 113; image of, 37; as male, 114; as mystery, 112; spiritual reality of, 119; wrath of, in Revelation, 89
gospels, as early Christian proclamation, 80-81, 84
grace, God's, 78, 95-97, 101, 117, 119
gravitation, law of, 38
Greek, koine, 25

Hebrews, book of, 92
Heidegger, Martin, 85
Hellenistic culture, 25, 27
Herodotus, 19

historicism, 31, 111
historicity, 28, 31
history, critical, 80
Hobbes, Thomas, 76
Homer, 18
homoousios, 27
Hubble, Edwin, 42
humanities, 30

ideas of faith, as product of human history, 112, 115
idolatry, 114
images, graven, 113
imagination, 29-30, 86, 113
intellect, role of, in faith, 120
Isaiah, book of, 92
Islam, 105
Israel, ancient, 18, 27, 113

James, William, 111
Jefferson, Thomas, 62
Jesus, 58, 79-97; actual words of, 83-84; as atoning sacrifice, 92, 94; biblical images of, 79, 100; existential significance of, 85, 86, 89, 90; as fully human and fully divine, 79; of history, 80, 85; as a Jew, 91; as living spirit, 85, 97; in non-Christian sources, 82; as son of God, 87
Jesus Seminar, 83 n. 2
John, Gospel of, 27 n. 3, 81, 88, 97
Johnson, Elizabeth A., 58
Josiah, 71
Jowett, Benjamin, 70
Judaism, 27, 70, 87, 105